Seven Years in Tuscany

IL BORRO

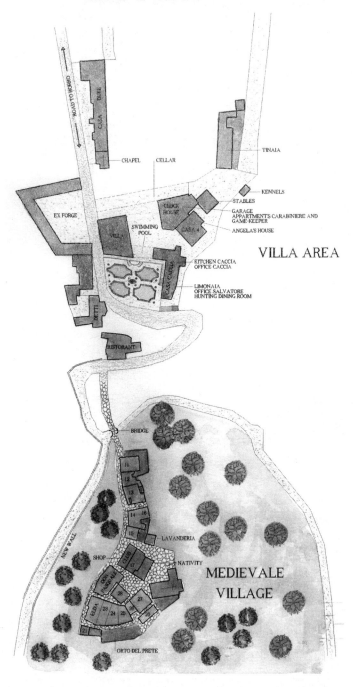

ROAD TO BORRO

CASA DUKE

TINAIA

CHAPEL   CELLAR

KENNELS

STABLES

GARAGE
APPARTMENTS CARABINIERE AND
GAME-KEEPER

EX FORGE

CLOCK
HOUSE

ANGELA'S HOUSE

VILLA

SWIMMING
POOL

CASA 4

VILLA AREA

KITCHEN CACCIA
OFFICE CACCIA

LIMONAIA
OFFICE SALVATORE
HUNTING DINING ROOM

DETTI

RISTORANT

BRIDGE

11
12
13

14   16

15

LAVANDERIA

NEW WALL

SHOP

CLUB
17

NATIVITY

MEDIEVALE
VILLAGE

18

26

27

ELDA
23   24   25   28   29   20

21

ORTO DEL PRETE

Seven Years in Tuscany

By Amanda Ferragamo

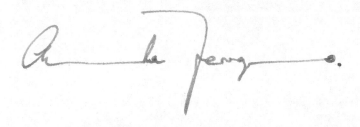

continuum
LONDON • NEW YORK

Continuum
The Tower Building
11 York Road
London SE1 7NX
www.continuumbooks.com

370 Lexington Avenue
New York
NY 10017-6503

First published 2002

British Library Cataloguing-in-Publication Data
A catalogue record for this book is available from the British Library.

ISBN 0-8264-6430-0

Typeset by YHT Ltd, London
Printed and bound by Bookcraft (Bath) Ltd

Contents

Acknowledgements

I would like to thank Michael Gunningham for his support and patience in guiding me through the first steps towards having this book published and encouraging me on my way.

My thanks also to Curt Baldwin who typed the manuscript with infinite patience and sat for many hours trying to make sense of what I had written by hand.

Finally I want to thank my publisher, Robin Baird-Smith, for all his skill and kindness and for having faith in me as an author.

Foreword

I went to see the Borro fairly soon after Amanda and Ferruccio had bought it. The medieval village – a church, small central square, village hall and about 20 houses – sits in a heaped jumble on top of a small hill or outcrop at the head of a valley in the hills running down from Florence to Arezzo. The main house or 'villa', with its cluster of smaller houses, farm and storage buildings and yards, overlooks the village at the end of the upland plain before it descends into the valley. The two, village and villa, are linked by a narrow, high vaulted stone bridge spanning the deep ravine between them.

The place was magical, but neglected and forlorn. Times had changed, and most of the inhabitants had gravitated to San Giustino, a village three or four kilometres away with modern housing and easy access by car and bus, and the majority of the houses in Il Borro were empty and derelict or in a poor state of repair. The villa too was largely unoccupied, half of it missing, having been blown-up by the retreating Germans in 1944 to block the road below.

The amount that needed to be done, in scale and complexity, was daunting. Neither Amanda nor Ferruccio had any significant experience of restoring old buildings or of land management and I wondered whether they fully appreciated what they were taking on. Perhaps not, but fortune (in her better moments) favours the brave and they set about the task with energy and enthusiasm, Ferruccio mainly addressing the farming and land-related aspects, for example the reintroduction of vines and improving the shooting, and Amanda the huge task of repairing all the buildings.

The vision was not only to restore the village and house, but to breathe life back into them so that they became once again a balanced and self-sustaining community. For example, Ferruccio insisted that at least some of the land should be farmed in the traditional way using yoke and oxen and Amanda, in restoring the village, ensured that the previous workshops were reinstated and used by traditional craftsmen with some, at least, of their produce sold in the newly established village shop.

This book tells how the vision was realised, in particular by Amanda, and how she devoted herself, and her considerable talent, charm, tenacity and creativity, to the task for the best part of seven years. As her brother, I am full of pride and admiration for her and for all she did at the Borro.

As it happens, this book, in its concept and execution as well as in its narrative, shows how she did it. She has never written a book before and had never been considered, by her brothers at least, particularly 'handy with the pen'. However, she said that she wanted to write down the story of the renaissance of Il Borro and undaunted by fraternal doubts and a lack of any relevant experience, she just got on and did it. Here is the result. I very much hope that everyone else enjoys the story as much as I did.

Michael Peat, August 2002

Introduction

The light dimmed and the orchestra started to play Glenn Miller's 'Chattanooga Choo Choo'. There was a gasp from a table in the far corner. A little girl had been sleeping slumped against the arm of her chair, legs dangling. The sudden darkness and the music woke her to a wonderland. What magic was this? She gazed at the band unbelievingly. The colours, the glitter, the heavenly light and most of all the music drew her like a magnet. Pudgy feet entrapped in shining patent Startrites squeaked as she wriggled to the floor, and with a few hesitant steps to the next table, her fat little hands lifted to rest on the edge, she gazed at the spectacle in front of her. Eyes like saucers, full mouth dropped open. 'Oh, oh, how pretty.' A few more waddling steps to the next table. The little round figure, in her tartan dress with its smocked bib, was drawn on and on. 'Oh, how pretty.' Closer and closer till she was standing in the light. It was real! A trombonist suddenly stood up and she jumped back in fright, hands flying to her hair. Her full skirt swirled. 'Oh, how pretty.' Her pudgy feet began to move, the skirt swirled wider and wider, fat arms were lifted above her head, she was taking off with the music, round and round. A strong arm broke the spell, a face looked down at her, 'Mummy!'

1

I was that little girl, two-and-a-half years old, and this was the first day of a new life for us all.

I was born at Burton House in Stockton-on-Tees in Durham, and had lived the first two years of my life in a house by the river called Ovington Edge, an ideal spot, peaceful and quiet, a country retreat where my mother and grandmother had fled during the war. My two elder brothers were born here too. Christopher, six years older than me, and David three. Living by the river, the sound of lively water racing over its rocky bed was constantly with me when dropping off to sleep, when waking in the morning. A background accompaniment to my daily life. The river was ever present with its different moods, slowly ebbing and lapping, or rushing and gurgling as if bursting with laughter, or angrily hissing and exploding as the water collided with the rocks on its mad rush to the sea. The sheep in the hills bleated, and horses clopped past on the lane. These were the sounds that were part of my tiny life until that night. Glenn Miller woke me to a different world.

My mother and my stepfather were starting off on their new life together. I was going with them, being too young to be sent away to school. My father, James Collingwood, a young subultern in the Army, had been wounded two months after landing in France on D-Day. His convalescence had been long and slow; now he was leaving for post-war Germany. This was at the beginning of 1949, and I didn't really see him again until he returned to England in 1954.

We lived in a little house in Petersham near Richmond Park, Daddy, (I have always called my stepfather Daddy), my old aunt Constance, my brothers and I, but now there was a new member of the family, my brother Michael. We have always been very close, Michael and I, and until I went away to boarding school two years later, we shared a room and a German nanny called Ernestine Iggle. Miss Iggle taught us nursery rhymes in German that I can still remember today.

My next clear memory is my first day at boarding school. Feeling strange in my new uniform, a five-year-old with dark hair caught in pigtails either side of my face with a green hat perched on top. Yatley Hall had a long driveway leading up to an old white house, long and low. I can't remember my first impressions of the building, my mind was in such a fog of fear and apprehension. I do remember crowds of people, trunks, and other little girls crying and saying goodbye. I clung to my mother's hand, hot and sweaty. Standing at the front door with my face pushed against the glass to get the last glimpse of the car as it disappeared, engulfed by the great oak trees aligning the drive, I distinctly remember seeing a large tin of Quality Street, on the back shelf, all its brilliant colours gradually fading – my mother had forgotten it. I don't remember crying, not then. I turned around, the hall was cavernous in the dying light, no one was around. 'Where have they all gone? Where do I go?' There was a magnificent wooden staircase leading upwards, with a huge window on the landing looking out over a moat, moorhens and wisteria. I started to climb these. It was ominously dark above, and I stopped halfway, uncertain. So I just sat on the steps. In front of me there was a picture of a lady with long dark hair and a sweet smile illuminated by the dying light from the window. I stared at her, concentrating on her face until it was imprinted on my mind. It wasn't until many years later that I discovered she was the Mona Lisa. She came back into my life many years later when I was a mother with children of my own. Eventually, I was found by the matron. 'Everyone has been looking for you,' she said, leading me into the refectory. The light and the noise of two hundred girls eating and chatting was devastating for a five year old. I was placed at a long wooden table next to a nun in a black habit. My life in a convent college had begun. It would last eleven years.

I slept in a room with three other little girls of my age, with a nun behind a screen. That night I wet my bed and soon after, the nightmares began. 'Awake nightmares' I called them, because they came before I was really asleep – in that lapse of time between two worlds. The sheets on my bed would gradually become heavy and cold like marble, the walls of the room breathed in and out and voices gibbered at me from all directions. I knew what was about to happen because pins and needles gradually crept into my fingers, and then I was gone – up out of bed and running. Nightdress flying down the long corridors of the school with a trail of nuns after me. They were mostly in just their underbonnets and dressing gowns, which was even more terrifying than seeing them in their black garb. These nightmares stayed with me right into early adulthood. I remember the feeling coming over me once when I was a seventeen-year-old, painting with great concentration in Florence. As I grew older, I managed to control the urge to run. The bed wetting problem was finally solved by Matron, with a clever bribe. She took me to see a litter of baby rabbits at a nearby farm, telling me I could choose one and take it home at the end of the term if I didn't wet my bed. The rabbit lived to a ripe old age in our garden at Petersham.

Dyslexia was unknown in those days. Was she backward? What is wrong with her? She is eight years old and still can't read and write. I was the oldest and tallest child in my class. Mandy. I was a veteran with a permanent black blob. Every

Sunday evening in the refectory, conduct marks were read out in front of the whole school. Gold stars, silver stars or the infernal black blob, my permanent status. Running in the corridors, talking after lights were out and arguing, that was my downfall. 'How can you put the lights out, Mother, at six-thirty on a Sunday evening? How are we meant to sleep in broad daylight?' and so on and so forth. A pugnacious brat, streetwise in convent life. Most evenings I was put in the corridor outside the dorm while the nuns walked up and down the cloisters below, saying their evening prayers. Sitting on the cold floor, I could hear the low drone of their chanting. There were mice around but I loved the little creatures. I had many pet mice which I kept in my pockets at home. On a few occasions I was forgotten, and once silence reigned again I would creep back to my bed. The only other major memory of primary school was ballet lessons. My mother was worried about my height, that I might begin to stoop, so she insisted I did ballet. I was a comical sight, totally unsuited for ballet. Towering above the other girls, robust and strong, I looked like Walt Disney's Hippopotamus in a pink tutu. Once we did a performance of the cygnets from *Swan Lake*. In our little white tutus, stretched out in a line with our arms crossed, we danced onto the stage. Thank goodness it was the dress rehearsal. In the front row was Father Dumphy, a Jesuit priest from my brother's school at Beaumont. There was a stifled groan, coughing and spluttering. He finally had to get up and walk out red in the face. The sight of me in the middle of this graceful, dainty line of little dancers had been too much for him. In the next performance I was relegated to being a tree, 'gracefully' waving in the wind at the side of the stage. As I said, I was not made to be a ballet dancer, but I continued with lessons all through school. I do, however, stand up straight.

At thirteen I moved to upper school at Farnborough Hill, not far away near Camberley. My father James had come back into my life and I spent part of my holidays with him, mostly at Army headquarters. I remember one holiday in particular at Brancepeth Castle in Durham. It was a great beast of a place, crouching like a prehistoric frog ready to pounce. It once had a moat, but that was now dry. Towers with arrow-slits guarded the archway into the central courtyard where peacocks strutted. The were dungeons where hideous torture had taken place in the Middle Ages, or so my brother explained to me, and ramparts where ghosts wander in lonely contemplation. Except, of course, when the boys went up to the roof to catch pigeons. I went, too, as the representative of the RSPCA. My brothers would shine a torch into the pigeons' eyes and, blinded, they would stay immobile. I, instead, would try to scare them off. It's a wonder we didn't all fall and break our necks.

My father was a major by now, and walked with a swagger stick. As we entered the castle through the archway the sentries would salute, stamping their feet on the cobbles. When my father saluted back, I did the same, it seemed the only polite thing to do. It must have been difficult for my father to deal with a little girl, especially one that had nightmares, in a wholly male environment. I did, however, have one redeeming quality – I could ride fearlessly. This pleased my father who was a great horseman himself. Once he bought a big hunter from a farmer up in the Dales. It was a freezingly cold morning in the Christmas holidays. The yard at the farm was covered in ice. A big bay gelding was brought out. The major mounted, and turning jumped him almost from a standstill straight out of the yard over a five-bar gate. Riverman, a horse I will never forget. Daddy (James), hired me a pony called Sputnik, a daring little beast

I had no control over, especially when he got the bit between his teeth out hunting. My father would indicate an open gate for me as he galloped off towards a large hedge, but Sputnik would have other ideas. If you have ever thought that Thelwell was a comic exaggeration of reality, believe me, he is true to life. Sputnik and I would careen towards the hedge, my father just a dot in the distance, and leap like a cat for the top. Here we would squirm and wriggle, I hanging on to his neck, hard hat over my eyes and pigtails flying. Once his front feet hit the ground he kicked out with his back legs until we were on all four feet. Then off after the others flat out, stomach to the ground, nostrils flared. Thelwell must have been there! My father would scold me on the way home, with a certain pride, 'You've got to have more control over that animal.' I, in my turn, would scowl, sending black looks in Sputnik's direction. 'I told you to take the gate. Now I have to spend hours medicating the scratches on your tummy!' The major has lived nearly all his life in the north. He is now retired and lives with his wife Constance in a little house overlooking the dales.

Farnborough Hill was originally the Empress Eugenie's palace. A magnificent house, now inhabited by 300 school-girls between the ages of thirteen and eighteen years. I was never good at schoolwork, and spent most of my time painting and taking main male parts in theatrical productions. Shakespeare and Gilbert and Sullivan, mostly. Farnborough was far stricter than the preparatory school. Silence was kept everywhere – we could only speak when given permission at lunch and supper. No running anywhere, all our letters in and out were opened, and we could only read books from the library. We wore thick lisle stockings with a suspender belt; there were no tights in those days. Heavy cotton pants in dark green with elastic around the legs. Mass was held every morning at six-thirty which we attended wearing a white-net veil and in the evening there was a rosary and benediction. From all this stricture and constriction, my mother sent me to Florence in Italy at the age of sixteen. She had always loved Italy, the colours enchanted her and thinking how I loved to paint, she sent me to the finishing school Le Fleuron. My mother's name is Dodo, a derivative of Josephine. She is certainly a rare bird, not extinct but certainly never to be repeated, only one of a kind. Fun-loving, beautiful with sparkling blue eyes, always ready for an adventure and eternally young. My stepfather, Sir Gerrard Peat, is the essence of an accountant and a gentleman. He taught me to keep accounts, and I still do to this day. My brothers have all gone their own way. Christopher, my eldest brother, is an accountant too, David is a stockbroker and Michael is Keeper of the Privy Purse and Treasurer to the Queen.

Florence was the beginning of my life in Italy. I met Ferruccio at Le Fleuron, owned and run by the Contessa de Germany. The Contessa invited young men from good families to meet the girls at her various soirées. We were allowed out three times a week, on Wednesday and Sunday until 10.30 p.m. and on Saturday until midnight. I met Ferruccio on one of these evenings and fell in love. Nothing else existed for me and when my mother insisted I went back to England to do the London season, I went, but with no enthusiasm or will to make a success of it. As far as I was concerned, I had found the other half of myself. The irony of the situation is that although I often went into a ball by one door and left by another, or perhaps because of it, I was voted Deb of the Year 1965. After the voting had been done by a group of debs, me included, the most photographed and publicised that year, a journalist interviewed the lot of us together in Tom Hustler's studio. I remember it very well. All the girls there knew I found the season a waste of time, I just wanted to get back to Italy. I worked in the morning as a mother's help taking a little girl to the park. Half asleep, I would wander around in a daze. On the rare evenings I was free I would cook dinner parties for my friends. All to earn money for my telephone calls to Florence and Ferruccio. At some point that evening after the voting, a journalist from the *Evening Standard* came over to question me. 'Did I enjoy doing the season?' I was wary. Where was this coming from? Who had been gossiping? I assured her I did and that it had been a main ambition in my life. This was way over the top, of course; the other girls tittered or turned away. What an unsophisticated lot we were, completely naive. Later that evening while the journalist was interviewing someone else, one of my friends asked me what would happen if I said what I really thought of the season. 'Personally,' I said, 'I would be hung, drawn and quartered.' This is what was written in the newspaper the next day:

> ONE MAN'S DEBS OF THE YEAR
> Miss Amanda Collingwood said she didn't like being a debutante really 'but I have to say I enjoy it or my mother will hang, draw and quarter me.'

The following September I went back to Italy, ostensibly to study for art college. Ferruccio and I were officially engaged to be married on 29 July 1967. There were the usual round of events, his family came to England, and my family to Italy. There were the usual articles in the newspapers. 'Ightham girl to wed Italian shoe designer's son', 'Italian fiancé for Miss Amanda Collingwood', 'Salvatore Ferragamo's son engaged.' But it never happened like that.

That winter, at the beginning of November, Florence was flooded. The whole town was devastated. November is always a rainy month but that year it didn't stop. There were frequent warnings about the dangerous height of the river Arno. Every morning there were the same dark skies, and every night I went to sleep to the sound of falling rain. The heavy skies continued to cover the earth with relentless water. Cars churned up wakes of water like motorboats, the garden was waterlogged. Two rivers of water gorged their way down either side of the road from Fiesole. The drains were blocked, water spouted forth like fountains everywhere you looked; and yet the sky was still laden. The bark of the trees was black and sodden, not a leaf was left on the branches. Normally, November is a month full of colour as the leaves turn and fall. The woods and the vineyards are full of autumn contrast; but not that year. The gutters over-flowed, sending continuous cascades of water pouring down the side of the house. Florence was in deep mourning. We gathered around the fire in the evening, worried faces asked: when would it stop?, how much more can it rain? There had never been anything like it before and hopefully there never will be again. Then one morning we woke up to silence; no rain, just the sound of dripping, endless, relentless dripping. The voice of the news broadcaster could be heard from below. 'Florence is flooded, the Arno has broken its banks.' We were all incredulous. What did it mean? How much? Where? Ferruccio and I drove down the hill and came to a stop in the middle of a bridge over the railway. All the buildings had lost their ground floors. No doors, no shops or bars, no petrol pumps, road signs or bus stops. The roofs of cars bobbed up and down, twisted and turned. Rubbish of every conceivable type floated by. Just yellow-brown brackish water swirled by in circles, laced with oil in strange hues of black and navy. It was so much like a dream. The water lapped past windows. Most were tightly shuttered but on higher floors people stood and stared in complete silence; just an occasional voice called, echoing across the water. It was a major catastrophe. The whole world was horrified, Florence, the city of art, was submerged in water.

'Water, water everywhere and not a drop to drink.' There had never been a truer word. A deluge had inundated Florence, she sat steeped in it and yet there was no drinking water, or any other type of useful water for that matter. We had crowds of people coming up to Fiesole with every form of container begging for water. We were lucky in many ways, and one of them was our water supply. We had our own source which enabled us to help others. It took many months of cleaning and digging out the mud to bring Florence back to any semblance of what she had been. For the works of art it would take years.

Both the Ferragamo headquarters at Palazzo Ferroni and the factory in Via Mannelli were on the river. The damage was extensive, and at that time a new factory was being built at the Osmannoro near the airport. My future mother-in-law, Wanda Ferragamo, asked me to postpone the wedding until a more settled time. Wanda is an extraordinary woman, dynamic with an amazing energy; her whole life has been dedicated to business and her family.

It wasn't until 15 May 1971 that Ferruccio and I were married on a beautiful day in Fiesole. The little church at Maiano was overflowing with guests, the English in hats, while the Italians stood out in their elegant simplicity. It was a glorious day, sunny and hot. After the reception in the

11

garden, Ferruccio and I drove to Naples where we spent the night at the Excelsior Hotel – in the same room his mother and father, Salvatore, had on their wedding night.

We lived in a little house by the gates in Fiesole, next to my mother-in-law. It had originally been a barn and storage for fodder. Renovated, it now had two bedrooms upstairs with a sitting room-cum-dining room, and a study. Downstairs there were garages, a kitchen and a service bedroom. The twins arrived and then Vivia; within twenty-five months I had three children. Learning how to be a multiple mum at short notice is not easy and I made many mistakes. Some funny, some not so much.

I had a Fiat shooting brake always loaded down with children, dogs and groceries. Not a good combination. The twins were about two-and-a-half years old, both strapped into their chairs in the back seat. I had to keep them as far apart as possible or they would either untie each other or, worse, fight. On this occasion we were driving home along the river loaded down with shopping. The boys were bored and fractious. I'd stopped a couple of times already to resettle them back in their chairs. I was close to losing my patience when I saw a man selling balloons at the side of the road. 'Ah, just the thing to keep them occupied.' I bought two, a red one and a yellow one, and anchored the string to their fat little wrists. It did the trick; they bobbed the balloons up and down on the roof of the car all the way home. The rest of the day was uneventful and at the usual hour they went to bed, still attached to their balloons. Later on, I went in and untied them. The balloons floated up to the ceiling and rested there.

The next morning nothing had changed, the balloons were still there nestled against the ceiling, cords just out of reach. I put the boys on their pots in the bathroom next door. The bathroom was long and narrow with a window at the end. It was so narrow that the boys sat under the lip of the basin, protected by the bath. Even on their pots it was impossible to keep them still. I thought of the balloons; perhaps they would work again. I gave them one each and continued dressing Vivia. Suddenly, there was an earth-shattering explosion, then silence. A few seconds passed and then all hell broke loose. All three children were screaming and shouting and there was cursing outside in the courtyard. I flew to the bathroom, Vivia yelling hysterically in my arms, terrified at what I might find. The boys were still sitting on their pots, completely covered in flakes of plaster and paint. The window was gone, blown out into the courtyard, and the curtain hung in shreds. The balloons had been filled with gas and had exploded on the heating element in the ceiling. If I had been wiser, the fact that the balloons were still fully blown up and attached to the ceiling should have told me something. But it never crossed my mind. The boys had a very lucky escape. The incident, however, influenced them for some years to come. First of all, when I tried to get them back into the bathroom sometime later that day, there was no way they would pass through the door. No way! Arms and legs thrust out, they were not going back in there. I made a makeshift bathroom in the bedroom. About a year later I took them all to the circus. We had a box right in the front. The clowns came in with orange wigs flapping up and down as they walked in their baggy trousers covered in patches. Enormous flat shoes sending sand flying up around them. Their painted smiles and red noses and finally the battered old car. Nothing had phased the boys so far and the girls were entranced. Suddenly the car let off a huge bang from the exhaust area, followed by clouds of smoke. In the silence that followed, two young voices, tight with fear, could be heard yelling: '*Scappiamo*.'[1]

The boys were up and gone, running up the steps to the exit. Panic is infectious and very soon half the children and their parents were making for the exit, not sure what had happened, only that they wanted to get out into the open. The circus organizers were furious, needless to say. The last time the boys bolted was at the Science Museum in London. They were about nine and fascinated by everything, the space shuttle in particular. We were high up on a stand when a 1000-watt electrical device exploded. Again it was a deafening bang; apparently there had been a warning over the loud speaker but in all the confusion I hadn't heard it. I was lucky, and a guard at the door stopped the boys running into the street. It is true most accidents happen in the home, even from something as trivial and banal as buying balloons. Very soon after, the twins started shooting with their father – and that was the end of the fear of big bangs.

My life was very simple and routine: children, house, garden, husband and family. A few years later, Olivia and then Vicky arrived. We spent our summers at our house by the sea and, as a rule, a few weeks or days during the winter in the family apartment at Cortina. I travelled with my husband on business. It was a privileged life. As the family grew we needed more space and expanded into the garages, then eventually to the other side of the courtyard.

This is a very brief account of my life up to the time this story begins. I have written it mainly to give a background to the future story and to give some idea as to where I came from.

* * *

1. 'Run for it'

Introduction

Ferruccio had for some time, I think as far back as 1985, owned 25 per cent of the shares of the Borro estate with his brother Leonardo. At this point, from what I understood, His Royal Highness Amadeo, the Duke of Aosta, wanted to sell all the rest of it, all the buildings, everything – except for his present house, which was the ex-factor's house. It was a long, pretty building exactly opposite the front door of the Borro villa itself, with the adjacent land around it and the swimming pool which was just across the road connected by a bridge. Leonardo consigned his share to Ferruccio. This was seven years ago and where this story begins.

1 Getting Started and Finding my Way

When we arrived at the main gates, we took a left down a track, quite a wide track; two cars could pass – just! On the right-hand side there was a high mesh metal fence, and running along in front of it there was a line of cypress trees. The original type of cypress tree, like a feather with its tip stuck in the ground; the others had a skirt like a semi-open umbrella. Underneath, there was heavy undergrowth, bushes and brambles. Behind this wire fencing, you could occasionally see an ostrich moving stealthily along the fence, with its long neck curved at an impossible angle and unblinking, curious eyes wondering who we were. On the other side of the track there was thick, heavy undergrowth with lots of scrub and bushes, with pine trees in groups here and there and an occasional oak. You could see that there were other animals behind the mesh fence; goats, sheep, lots of deer – big deer, fallow deer – and a large white grey crane. There was a lake in the centre. But all this I noticed over time, not on that first day.

Continuing along the track we passed a little red house, more of a pink colour really, on the right, and on the left there was a type of shack with open sides and a wooden, falling down roof, an old rally car complete with number, a wooden cart and other types of farm equipment. On the right again, there was another long structure, the *tinaia*[1] that was part of a group of tumbledown farm buildings.

Turning a sharp corner between two buildings, we suddenly found ourselves face to face with the villa. It was the first time I had seen the villa close up. A wave of sadness swept over me; it was forgotten and falling apart. Stuffing was falling out along the eaves of the roof, birds had made their nests in it and pigeons strutted up and down on the guttering. The wonderful stonework around the windows was cracked and crumbling. A few shutters were still in quite good condition but the plaster had come off in patches, leaving the brickwork exposed.

The villa had originally been a pink, peachy colour – you could see it in various places under the roof overhang, or at the front of the house, under the stone archways. Here the colour was still vibrant. For a short while I stood there and looked at it, then bells began to chime. There were two large bells on the roof of the villa – or what was left of it. The big bell chimed the hour, while the smaller one toned the minutes.

I can't remember the exact time of year, but I think it must have been sometime around February. It definitely wasn't warm, it was a cold, dark, windy day, and it must have been the early hours of the afternoon. A middle-aged man, quite small, with a balding head and grey hair, suddenly appeared and asked if we had permission to be there. We said we had, and we also had permission to see inside the house and that my husband, Ferruccio Ferragamo, would like to show me around. He smiled and turned away to find the keys. Meanwhile Ferruccio explained to me who the man was: Giovanni Ciprianni, administrator and accountant for His Royal Highness The Duke of Aosta.

1. winery

17

Giovanni was a solid presence in my life and my work at the Borro from that day forward. Little and wily, with a shining pate and fringe of grey hair, he stood with military bearing, always elegant and soberly dressed; a touch of the suave, with a pullover thrown around his shoulders. He would jump to attention and salute me on my frequent daily visits to his office. He had, in his youth, been in the army and did everything at a trot; surrounded by telephones and computers, he would rule his domain with sharp orders while scratching his head. In the village he was known as 'grattuga', (grater), as in cheese. I'm sure he knew this but never let on. He was generous and kind and looked after his old father of ninety with dignity and humour – the latter was in great demand when dealing with me. 'You can't buy materials for the Borro with your Amex, Signora!'

'I'm so sorry Giovanni.'

'I'll fix it for you this time.' A few days later he would be running across the courtyard shaking a bunch of invoices in his hand: 'Signora, Signora, these you have put on your personal Visa.'

'Oh Giovanni, so I have.'

There was a side door, let's say a side entrance without a door but with a metal roll-door as you would see in a shop. This was unlocked. Straight in front of us there was a very steep set of stairs with a low roof going downwards. We turned left up two steps and along a corridor with long windows. From these windows the other face of the villa was all too evident. Like the *Phantom of the Opera*, this elegant villa bore the waste of war and weather in isolated cruel disfigurement, dominating the village below it with its craggy frown, house birds and sighing winds that rushed up the valley. I realised the enormity of the work in front of me, but at the same time I was glad it had fallen to me. In a way, it was poetic justice. During the war the Allied forces advancing on the road below caused the German soldiers left behind to mine the villa. Almost half of it tumbled onto the road in a mass of rubble and dust. Having been destroyed to prevent the British and American advance, it seemed only right to me that an Englishwoman would embrace the villa's renaissance.

The house stands in a prominent position facing down a valley formed by five small rivers, in the centre of which, at the pointed end of the wedge forming this spur of land, there is an island culminating in a medieval village – Il Borro.

Because of the shape of the land, the house is irregular on all sides. The side facing the village to the south has four floors. The roadside has six floors. The front facing the chapel and north has two. The last side facing the courtyard, three. This is the only side with a mezzanine. These architectural discrepancies could be verified by old photos of the house taken before the war. Now all that was left was an L-shape including the front and the courtyard side. There were no photos to tell me what the inside had originally been like.

Ferruccio and I made a tour of the house. There wasn't much to see. The remaining L-shape on the ground floor consisted mainly of rooms piled with packing cases and boxes. Giovanni had his office at the end of the long corridor looking over the Borro village. The short side of the L at the front of the house had a couple of rooms and a bathroom, plus a study on the right of the entrance. This configuration was roughly repeated on the second floor, or would-be top floor.

Below the ground floor at the courtyard and entrance level, there was a jumble of rooms, staircases and corridors, some leading out to the garden at the back, others right

19

down to the cellar and finally across the remaining rubble to a wooden door leading onto the village road.

There were two interesting features. One was the entrance hall. It had a very high ceiling, about two metres higher than the rooms converging on it from the corridor. There was only one flight of narrow stone stairs that twisted and turned their way up this side of the house, with quaint oval windows on small landings. Emerging at midway up the stairs we found a strange kind of mezzanine floor. This was the second interesting point. It only existed down the long side of the L, and always had according to the photograph, with much smaller windows, and ceilings I could touch with my fingertips. The house began to make sense to me and to come together in my mind. The reason for the diversification in ceiling heights was now obvious. Where had the main staircase been? More to the point, as I began to plan its renovation in my mind, where would it fit best in a family home?

The last area to investigate was up the stairs, yet again, right into the loft. Here the eaves were low and there was not much to see, a bit of rubbish here and there, boxes, bottles and books. We climbed through a small door, up wooden steps and out onto a long, narrow terrace. On this terrace were the two big bells I mentioned earlier. They began to chime. The noise was deafening. I turned and looked around me; the view was almost 365 degrees, and there was an emptiness below me where there was nothing left of what must have once been a magnificent house.

The valleys ran away to the south mostly surrounded by woodland and those strange *balze*[1] of yellow clay that are so

1. crags

typical of this area. A dip in the hills gave you a peek of the *campanile*[1] at Castiglion Fibocchi.

To the north, the Pratomagno stood out clearly in profile against the cold sky. Snow lay in patches and drifts on peaks towards Loro Ciuffenna. On one side of the villa, there were fields, vineyards and farmhouses, mostly uninhabited, nestled into the gentle slopes to the left. To the right there was a high plateau, more fields, vineyards and an airfield. Large navigation balls danced on the electricity wires and the chuckle of pheasants was distinct in the distance. The emptiness of the ruined side yawned below me. It must have been a fine house in its day. This was my introduction to the Borro, and as first impressions go, it was a good one. I felt excited and feverish with ideas.

Word of mouth is about the only way to find good workmen. We were now looking for a firm of builders to begin the work. The Borro was essentially a shooting reserve at that time. There are something like six million people living in Italy who have a licence to shoot game and unless the land has been granted a reserve, a man with his gun and a dog can go just about anywhere. So you can imagine how important the gamekeeper was on our reserve. Our first job was to restore an apartment for the man who would hold this indispensable role.

I divided the project of restoring the property into three parts. One was the villa, with all its annexes, the *limonaia*, *granaio*, garages, pigsties, cellar, *tinaia*, gardens and entrances. The second was the working part of the estate: the medieval village and fifteen farmhouses, agriculture and its produce, shops, and so forth. The third was a plan passed

1. bell tower or steeple

21

down to us by the previous owner for a golf course and tourist village. All three of these goals had to be worked on at the same time and the job itself thought of as a whole. No part of the whole could be separated or the picture itself would not be complete – a very tasty morsel for a building firm.

The Borro project was a gift from heaven. I longed to use my ability to create, which had been dormant almost since I left school. Hard work and long hours had never been a problem. The only problem was combining the roles of mother, wife and housekeeper and, as time went on and work grew, some of my previous obligations were inevitably neglected.

My mother-in-law was kind and suggested we use a man called Paccini who had been working for her. We couldn't have been more fortunate. Paccini lives in our area at Terranuova Bracciolini and is a dynamo of energy and enthusiasm, small and tough, with a shock of black hair going grey at the sides and the complexion of a man who works outdoors. Alessandro, his son, works with him and is just a younger version of his father. No job was too difficult or too small for his complete attention. He would run from one task to another, trousers slipping down around his hips which he continually hitched up. One moment lugging a huge beam for a roof, the next mixing cement or making *tracce* – grooves for the plumbers and electricians.

We had the same ideas about the importance of building quality. A job done well, once. It didn't always happen, but as a team we worked well together. I always consulted him on the programmes first thing in the morning when we met at 7.30 a.m. to start the day. The first morning I think Paccini was surprised to see me. I don't think he expected me to be so involved in every aspect of the building process. I learned a lot from him, and he learned how to work with a woman and a foreigner. One morning I asked him why the *sogliole* had not yet been laid at doors. I saw a flash of real amusement cross his face. 'They're not fresh this morning, Signora.' He saw the puzzled response on my face and then of course he explained I had used the wrong word. *Sogliole* is sole and *soglia* is threshold! I have now learnt a lot of building words in Italian that I don't even know in English.

Another time there was a bit of rain. I found Paccini and all his men taking cover. 'Mr Paccini,' I said, 'in England if we stop because it rains, we would work one month a year! I suggest you put some plastic covering up.' This was another novelty for him but as always, ready to please, he complied. I could hear a few mumbles from the men but I kept smiling and as I was wet and muddy too, the work continued. Paccini had about ten men working for him. Gradually, over the weeks, I learnt all their names, what they were especially good at, and inevitably what problems they had with health or home. It was a good atmosphere. In the morning there was a chorus of 'Buongiorno, Signora.' I tried to remember to ask the right questions, and never moved a man from one job to another without consulting Mr Paccini first. Mr Paccini was always 'Mr Paccini', whereas the other work-men had nicknames or I simply called them by their first name. My only complaint, as far as Mr Paccini was concerned, was his willingness to please – everyone! I had to watch him like a jealous wife. Anyone could come by and lure him away at the drop of a hat. One moment he could be there, the next gone. I would return to a site that had been a hive of activity an hour before and he was nowhere in sight. I would call the second-in-command at that time Berlusconi.

'Where is Mr Paccini?'

'Stefano came by and they have gone to see a well, or a bridge in the riserva.'

'But if this work is not finished today, the plumbers cannot get in tomorrow, and everything will *salta*[1].'

A shrug of the shoulders from Berlusconi would say it all, and I would go storming off to look for him.

Our first crane went up in the main courtyard at the beginning of July. It was exciting. Work had begun. The entire roof of the clock house was removed and placed on the ground. By the beginning of October two apartments were ready, one for the gamekeeper and one for a *carabiniere*, who would keep an eye on things and be a deterrent against trespassers, especially at night. We had no gates or walls at this time.

The interiors were done in the traditional Tuscan fashion, terracotta on the floors, whitewashed walls and beamed ceilings with *campagiane*[2] in between. The structure of the roofs was done well with a framework of wood, followed by *campagiane*, meshing, cement, tarred sheeting, Styrofoam and finally roof tiles – all this in the hope of maintaining some heat in the winter months. The Borro can be very cold and windy, and as it is not on the gas mains we have to use bottled gas. More than one person in the area has complained that their gas bills are higher than the rent.

Most of the apartments I have restored over the years are small – two, at most three, bedrooms. There are certain things I consider important. On the practical side, a kitchen big enough to have an eating area, and an area away from the stoves for the washing machine. I also consider where the rubbish is going to be kept, and washing hung to dry. Good

1. fall apart
2. terracotta tiles

storage cupboards for groceries and cleaning equipment are important, as is a decent sized fridge; and all electric domestic equipment should be of top quality, easily serviced. Wherever I could, I have put in an airing cupboard, not only for linen but also for hanging wet coats, boots and hats when coming in from outside – strategically placed near the front door. Skirting boards are important and they need to be quite deep. I nearly always had these made in wood. They protect the wall when you are cleaning or waxing the floor but are also convenient for running wires or piping behind. On the decorative side, I like to use countrified tiles, bigger and heavier than the ordinary commercial types, and a lot of white with pretty borders to combine with the colour scheme in the adjoining rooms. For example, the decorative theme in the bathroom should be such that towels will match both or all of the bedrooms. When tiling any room, and especially when the tiles on the floor are perpendicular to those on the wall, where it's almost impossible to match up the grouting, I like to use a type of skirting board in tile. It can be a repetition of the finishing border, or just a simple, narrow, long tile that breaks the meeting point between wall and floor, making it more defined and clean cut. If I'm using wood in a kitchen for cabinets, I add a wooden skirting board. These are small details but I feel it is these that make a home complete.

Talking about detail, I suppose it is a fixation with me, but if certain details that make the picture complete are not correct, it gives the wrong feel to the whole house. After all, if you are going to take a job on you might as well do it properly. There was one instance that brought out this streak in me, which I think was a precedent for the future work I would undertake.

There is a garage under the clock house which I imagine was originally used for carriages. On opening the big wooden doors, I was struck most of all by its vaulted ceiling. The entire space is divided by an arch, either side of which is vaulted to a central point. Having had the ceiling sand-blasted to remove the remains of damp and sodden plaster, the original vaults emerged. A masterpiece of detail and precision, small terracotta tiles converged on the central point in a herringbone pattern. The floor was simply cement – that is, what remained of it. Whatever this space had housed in the past, today we had to use it as a garage, which meant oil, exhaust marks and quantities of water. Obviously drains would be needed, and a slight grading of the floor so water would naturally drain away, preferably centrally placed. I could not use terracotta, didn't want to use cement, and finally decided to use klinker. Klinker is produced in a different size to terracotta, in smaller, thinner, rectangular tiles. Holding one in my hand, actually made in Germany, I looked up admiring the ceiling, then down again at the floor; it should, and could, be a reflection of the ceiling. The tile I had in my hand was almost the same size as the ceiling tiles. With a central drain as a converging point and four draining ruts leading to it, the floor mirrored the four segments created by the vaults. I divided the space in two at the arch with a piece of *pietra serena* the width of the lateral columns and used *pietra serena* again for the draining ruts converging on the central drain.

Now for the tiling. Mr Paccini found me an experienced man to do this and I explained in great detail what I wanted – the exact reflection of the ceiling. Unfortunately I had to be away for a couple of days, so was really excited to see the finished work. On my arrival at the Borro, I went straight to the garage. The last tiles were being washed down. The

26

impression was good, all glistening; the beautiful colours of terracotta and grey *pietra serena* combined were effective. As the floor dried my heart sank. I looked closer, I couldn't believe it. After all my explaining, the man had just laid the tiles straight up and down. I was stunned. With the pit of my stomach churning, I asked him why he had done it.

'Oh it's fine like this, Signora, in fact better. You see what a good effect it gives straight up and down.'

'But not the effect I asked for or wanted.'

'Oh well, it's done now.'

I took a deep breath and, keeping my voice in control, I quietly asked him to take it up and start again.

He couldn't believe it. 'Fifty square metres!' The finished product *was* stunning; all the hassle had been worth it. Even in a garage. I think I had made my point.

I had a series of carpenters who worked for me. Each one had his own speciality. I now met Donatello. Donatello has a factory at Faella, about thirty minutes away, and drives rather a nice Mercedes. He wasn't always that keen when I jumped in beside him followed by a muddy dog. Always the gentleman, he never let his annoyance show. He was tall and slim with slightly thinning hair, about mid-fifties, an expert at making windows and doors. We worked out a deal for the price of his work and in all the years we worked together it never changed. I would draw what I wanted done, not only in the way of doors and windows, but also built-in cupboards and shelves. He was always very complimentary about my drawings, however rough they were, pointing out details with the remains of a finger that had had an unfortunate clash with an electric saw. He also worked with his son Tommaso and his older brother Dino. But Donatello was definitely the energy and the verve behind it all. He was more than just a carpenter; he took an active interest in the council and activities of his local town. I would meet him occasionally at dinners or cocktails given by the local dignitaries. He was always very circumspect and attentive, especially if I was unaccompanied.

2 Horses and Dogs

By October the polo season is well and truly over. The ponies are put out to grass until the following spring. Salvatore, one of my twin sons and the first-born, and I turned up at Terry Hanlon's yard about the middle of that month. He wasn't immediately available so we wandered around the yard. The nameplates on some of the stable doors intrigued me – Zanuzzi, Hoover, Miele. Terry is an intriguing man himself, a real rough diamond who speaks his mind without a second thought. He commented almost immediately on my handbag made of ostrich skin, not from the Borro I hasten to add; on how handsome Salvatore was and why didn't he become a film star.

I had never met Terry before but I'd certainly heard him. He is famous for commentating at polo matches, and with his broad Cockney accent and his caustic sense of humour, very popular. Once I was watching a match at Cowdray in a large black straw hat, a black and white leopard print linen dress and high-heeled, sling-back sandals – totally useless for stomping back the sods of earth between games, but there you go, it's what's expected, and in fact it is quite fun in a contradictory way. The pony lines are full of steaming restless horses; the air pungent with the smell of their sweat and manure. Horses thunder past, shoulder to shoulder; men swear in Spanish and clods of grass spray earth in all directions. Champagne glasses clink with tumblers of Pimm's, people glance at each other in a surreptitious way, and greet friends in loud voices, 'Oh darling, how divine.' The backs of Land Rovers and Bentleys open to display picnics, silver candlesticks on rickety tables serving celery stalks and smoked salmon.

The English season swings. Shades of Ascot, Glyndebourne and the Fourth of June. We are experts at picnicking. No other nation can compete; we crown our sovereignty by always doing it in the most inappropriate clothes. Keeping our attention at sporting events is no small feat. To bring our minds back to the real purpose of the event there is the commentator – Terry is an ace!

Later on in the same year, I was fortunate enough to sit next to the Prince of Wales at a dinner. I asked him how he could possibly concentrate on his game with this type of commentary going on, wasn't it off-putting?

'Not at all,' he replied, 'it is all part of the game.'

We bought three ponies, my son Salvatore chose two and I chose one. The latter was small (about 14.3 hands), a dark bay with large intelligent eyes that seemed to have gone to a place beyond patience. She had a perfect round dent in her forehead; the fruit of a polo stick landed with force. I was given all the gory details by her owner. She was still the first in the scrum, pushing with all her weight, fleet of foot and capable of turning on a sixpence. She was now apparently twelve years old and in the last two years had worked with the pony club polo team. I had to have her. All was concluded with Terry and transport organised to Italy. As I left that day I looked back at the stable doors. Why the strange names? Perhaps the polo players' girlfriends or wives chose them. There might be something Freudian in that thought.

This was a real case of putting the cart before the horse. I had not looked for anyone to tend to the horses, nor started to build the stables and a place for the groom to live before the ponies arrived. By now it was cold, autumn was definitely giving way to winter. Thank God polo ponies live outside and we had one field which was fenced, big enough for many more than three horses. An old retired agricultural worker came every day on his bicycle to look after the ponies. He seemed to enjoy doing it, and twice a day he would wobble down the track. One evening he wobbled right off the track into the ditch. Poor Natale! He was pulled out by Alvaro, the farmer, who saw the bicycle wheel sticking up out of the ditch as he drove his little Panda home. I can still see him standing there in the beige-coloured overall he always used to work in, covered with a jacket against the cold, standing with his hands in his pockets staring down at Natale.

'What are you doing down there?' he asked slowly and thoughtfully. He would rub his forehead just above the brow and smile in a troubled way. I've seen him do it often when talking to me! Natale was not hurt, but he was shaken and stayed home for a few days.

I took over his duties for these days. This meant I had to stay at the Borro during the week for the first time. I kept all the dogs with me for company. There was Barden, Bliza, Brugo and Biga, all shorthaired German pointers – mother, father and their two children. I had to get the job done by 7.30 a.m. to start my day with Mr Paccini. I worked out a very good system, wrapped up like the Michelin man with only my eyes and nose exposed, the latter red and running as I stepped outside.

Once at the field, I would feed the horses and wait for them to finish, for Woody had long teeth and was a slow eater. If I didn't stay the others would take her food. The world is the same all over for man and beast. But this gave me a good ten minutes for the dogs to run and for me to walk around stamping my feet and banging my arms up and down like an obese bird trying to take off. They were good times though, with the air cold and crisp and the dogs frolicking around. One of the first things I did on those mornings was feed them. While they ate I fetched the pick-up truck and loaded it with buckets for the horse-feed. As soon as the dogs had finished I would load them on too, and off I would go with four faces looking at me through the back window, ears flapping. Sometimes there were the most beautiful sunrises and cloud formations I have ever seen. I learnt to tell, from which way the wind was coming, what type of day each particular sky foretold. I felt full of energy on those mornings and was almost sorry when Natale came back to take over.

3 Bonnie

Father Christmas came through the door pushing his hat back. 'Whew,' he smiled at me and his bright blue eyes sparkled over his bushy, white, cotton-wool beard. 'It's like an oven in here, how can you bear it?'

I lifted my eyebrows and looked at him: 'Thin blood.' I was tucked up in an armchair next to the fire. It was our first Christmas at the Borro, to be exact at Number 4. On my lap was a little black bundle; she was my Christmas present but she didn't come on a sledge from the North Pole. She came from a shop in Via Dei Servi in Florence and she was the last thing I had expected or in fact wanted – Bonnie.

Olly and Vicky, my two youngest daughters, and I had been Christmas shopping. I love Christmas and the atmosphere in Florence was especially Christmassy that year because it was so cold. We could see our breath puff before us as we walked. It was dark by now and all the lights in the decorations were flashing on and off. Tinsel in silver and gold, red berries and mistletoe. Christmas-time is magical in the evening with all the shop windows alight. People hurried by in boots and furs, with pink noses and steaming breath. We had been shopping most of the afternoon and were loaded down. Walking our way towards the garage past the Duomo there is a long street, Via Dei Servi, full of shops, lights and sparkle. Olly made to go down it. I remembered that halfway down there was a pet shop, to be avoided at all times but especially now.

'No Olly, not down there.'

Too late, she was off and made straight for the pet shop.

'No Olly, don't even look.'

Vicky and Olly stood with their noses pressed against the window.

'Come away, both of you,' I called from the other side of the road.

'Oh Mummy, look!' They turned and between them, behind the glass two black eyes looked straight at me.

Now she was sitting on my lap waiting for Father Christmas to finish his job for the evening. Stockings filled, it was time for his reward – biscuits and a glass of warm brandy left by the hearth.

'Are you going to have your drink?' I asked him.

'No thanks Mum, I'm knackered; I'm going to bed, Happy Christmas.'

Bonnie and I sat on looking into the fire. I drank the brandy and she had the biscuits. Had I thought of everything? I ticked them off in my head. Olly and Vicky would be up at dawn opening their presents. I tiptoed off to bed, and put Bonnie in her basket by my side.

Ever since I got married I have organised a major part of Christmas lunch, nearly always held at Il Palagio, the family home in Fiesole. This would be the first year it would be at the Borro. Our numbers had increased dramatically. There were now many grandchildren and great grandchildren. We always had *brodo*[1] to begin with, with special tortellini

---

1. clear soup

brought down fresh from Bologna by Beatrice, Leonardo's wife. I did the turkeys, stuffed with sausage meat, sage and onion at one end and chestnut and herbs at the other, as well as special crispy roast potatoes and mountains of gravy. Giovanna, my sister-in-law, always brought the salad and vegetables and my mother-in-law a multitude of sweets. The table was festive with red and gold damask cloth, gold candles, gold-rimmed crystal glasses and fine Spode china. Decorations of pomegranates, gold leaves, red berries and white roses, clustered around candles, made a real Christmas table.

My only offering here were the crackers sent over from London. Crackers are not used in Italy at Christmas as a rule, but I like to have them, especially for the children. I remember one year sitting there, everyone flushed and happy with their cracker hats on.

'Just think,' I said, 'everyone in England is sitting at this very moment with their paper hats on, too.'

Leonardo replied, 'Just think, Mandy, we are the only people in Italy wearing them!'

4 Getting to Know People, Number 4 and the Stables

Horses whinnied and stamped, dogs barked. The morning news floated up from the floor below. I turned over warm and cosy under the duvet, reluctant to open my eyes. Bonnie's wet nose snuffled in my ear. 'Wake up, wake up, it's time for breakfast.' Everyone seemed to be saying the same that Saturday morning in our new apartment at Number 4 Il Borro. Many projects had been completed: the stables, the groom's apartment and the garage that joined her new home with ours. This time with its original floor in slabs of old, ridged *pietra serena*. I had made an enormous kitchen at Number 4, straight up a flight of stone stairs from the front door. Men leaving their coats and guns at the bottom would walk into a wave of warmth flowing from the high open fire. A rosy glow flickered and danced its reflection on the tiled floor. From heavy beams hung a *giogo*[1] with lamps hanging at either end, and yellow and white chequered cushions were piled up on an old church pew. Yellow mugs hung from hooks on the *credenza*[2], antique Windsor

1. yoke
2. dresser

chairs clustered around a huge wooden table, two-and-a-half inches thick. Baskets were filled with onions and garlic. Pots of herbs scented the warm air, mingling with the smells of fresh baked bread, coffee and tobacco. Breakfast on a Saturday morning is my favourite time.

The stables had been difficult to build, mostly because of the difference in levels. From the block where we were now situated, the ground dipped sharply to the level of the cellar under the main courtyard. The stables were originally pig-sties and therefore the ceilings were low. Of the original structure there was very little left except for the actual dimensions. I could not go higher to achieve the height I needed for horses, so I went lower. By digging down and building a retaining wall, I managed to create a small courtyard in front of the groom's house with a round win-dow looking directly in on the horses. We filled this little courtyard with rambling roses, honeysuckle and jasmine. With its wrought iron table and chairs and pretty cushions, it became a secret garden. I could look down on it from my bedroom window and in spring and summer the scent of the flowers wafted up.

A small terrier is barking in the yard and 'Sex in the City' is blaring away on the television in the study and the sun is pounding through my window as I look out onto the breathtaking view of Florence. In my mind's eye I see a gummy grin, and a pair of jet-black eyes as Bonnie crabs sideways in the dance of delight she does when she sees me. Bonnie is not an original name for a Scottish terrier, the equivalent of Whisky if she had been a boy, but in my eyes she was original. As with most things that you don't want or don't want to do, she turned out to be the best of gifts. It was the absence of barking that brought Bonnie to mind.

Thinking about the building of the stables has reminded me of an incident when I nearly lost Bonnie. Bonnie is strange, as little dogs go, because she very rarely barks. It nearly caused her death this time, and eventually did. The groom's house, or Angela's house as it soon became known, was originally a cow byre. During the work that winter, and especially at the beginning while just planning its formation, it was pitch black inside with no fixed electric light. Bonnie was my shadow, my little black conscience, my greatest confidante and sounding block, but there were times when we forgot each other. I would be totally engrossed thinking about a job and drive off leaving her behind, and she would be too engrossed chasing lizards or catching mice, at which she was exceptional, or simply investigating smells to notice I had left. I felt quite sorry for the mice but I had to admire her technique.

On this particular day, my first job in the morning had been reviewing the site for Angela's house. The morning progressed in the usual manner but something was missing, nagging at the back of my mind continuously. By mid-morning while on my way to have a cappuccino it hit me – Bonnie. Where the hell was Bonnie?

Panic set in. Think carefully! Mezzogiorno came and the men arrived back for their lunch. They set out to help with the search. Everyone loved Bonnie, she was a mascot.

'Signora, Signora, I can hear a scuffling and scratching in the old cow byre but we've looked and we can't see her anywhere,' one of the men exclaimed.

We all gathered in the dark, musty room. There *was* a scuffling; it seemed to be coming from under the ground. Using the torchlight we covered the area inch by inch. In one corner there were some wooden planks partially covered with earth, with a small gap in the centre which enabled us to ease them up. An old *orcio*[1] had been buried in the ground, and sitting in the bottom was Bonnie. She looked sheepish and cold, and was shivering when I lifted her out. I heard someone say 'grazie al cielo'. (But why doesn't she bark?)

I think it is time I introduced you to the *architetto*. He, like Mr Paccini, has always been 'the *architetto*' even after years of work together every day. His actual name is Elio Lazarini. He was born, lives and works in San Giustino, our village. We met the first time to discuss the building of a wall between the Duke's garden and ours. This was done with mutual consent. With five children, the same number of dogs, four wheelers, go-carts, footballs and horses, it was difficult to maintain an invisible and retaining limit. The *architetto* is always very circumspect and stood to one side while we discussed exactly where the boundaries lay. It was decided that we would build the wall and we submitted a detailed drawing. The *architetto* is always elegant, almost too much so, at least in comparison with me! He is very tall and slim, with little hair but a lot of beard. He nearly always wears a hat. His manner is quiet and gentle. His hands are fine and small and his feet always clad in highly polished shoes. If we went to a building site he would remove his shoes and put on boots, rolling up his trousers to avoid getting them dirty. I saw him glance at my muddy shoes – that was before I began wearing strong workman's boots. I was always a mess, covered in dust and plaster and the inevitable mud.

I am biased where architects are concerned. I feel it is paramount for them to do things their way. Their reputation

1. a large terracotta pot used to hold oil

is at stake. I feel the same, but look at the situation from a different angle. In my usual way I told him this as nicely as I could, explaining that I had very clear ideas, but could not do the technical drawing, nor present them to the council concerned, by law, even if I had been capable. He looked at me with his kind and understanding eyes. He quite understood; if I did the sketches he would do his best to accommodate me. It was the beginning of a partnership and friendship that was infinitely precious and invaluable to me all the years of my work at the Borro.

Angela is Scottish, with a broad accent Ferruccio found impossible to understand. She came with her fiancé Tim Bell from Skipton in Yorkshire. Ferruccio was, by this time, completely confused. 'How do they understand each other?' They moved into their little house, bought a large TV set and video as their first priority and literally hundreds of Walt Disney tapes. Tim had followed Angela, and now we had to find him a job. We turned him into a bricklayer's mate. Angela had worked in a bank before and Tim as a printer so this was all completely new for them – a new life, new experiences and new jobs. Angela is small-boned and fair, with a temper. Tim was exactly the opposite in every way; big with dark hair balding at the temples and slow to anger. Ideal qualities for a bricklayer's mate. We teamed him up with Antonio from Sardegna. The Borro was becoming very cosmopolitan. In the bar at San Giustino, English was spoken in various hues and Italians stood back and watched with lots of tutting and clicking of tongues. The bar was called after the owner's wife, Marisa. She was certainly worth calling a bar after, in fact two. They had another one in Terranuova Bracciolini. She was petite but voluptuous with a Marilyn Monroe touch, very blonde hair, cleavage and perfect make-up.

Marisa did not exude friendliness. Every time I went in I would chat and smile but got very little response. Why? Perhaps it went with the territory? Her husband was big and jolly with a white apron tied round his waist in the French style, always ready to try a new recipe for his ice-cream. He proudly showed me around his laboratory of clinically clean white tiles with big shining metal vats continually churning the ice-cream. There was no place for miles that could compete. This was the genuine article, for which all Italy is famous. In the summer months, the square and the bar itself were packed until the late hours.

I always considered going to Marisa's as a reward for a morning's work. I looked forward to it. The *architetto* and I would roll up in his little green Panda, Bonnie at my feet. Strangely enough he never made any fuss about the mud and dirt Bonnie brought in, but she always stayed at my feet – she knew instinctively that this was the *architetto*'s car. In my car she always sat on the armrest between the front seats, ears pricked, eyes bright, twisting her head from side to side, taking in everything. If we passed another dog she would jump onto the seat and stand at the window, returning to her observation post once she had passed judgement on the unfortunate pedestrian. The *architetto* and I would order our coffees and sit down to warm our cold hands and feet while discussing projects and plans scattered around on the table. Bonnie had to stay outside, it's the law. We would be so involved in our thoughts and plans that, still engrossed in conversation, we would leave without her. Over the years she would get used to this and just make her way home, down the road and past the cemetery. If someone tried to intercept her progress, she would flash her gummy smile showing her sabre-like canines through her black beard. I thought she looked just like Captain Hook when she did this. But it deterred any well-meaning citizen and in time she became a well-known figure trotting along in her busy way. It was all quite routine. Marisa and I got to know each other over time. She is warm-hearted and sympathetic, often cheering me up on dark days when I felt I was getting nowhere.

5 The Entrance and Politics

Balls, yes balls, can be very frustrating, especially if you are not an expert. It is all a question of size, dimension and diameter. Actually it is a simple mathematical equation, a question of height and distance. I had been standing looking at pillars with a young man perched on top gripping a ball for some time, and I couldn't decide what was wrong. The first time I had come across this problem had been while constructing the boundary wall. I didn't want just a straight line, a Berlin copy with turrets and barbed wire, but something soft and graceful that would integrate with its surroundings. I decided to make the wall curved with capitals and balls at every other dip. The wall itself was plastered and painted the same peachy pink colour of the houses either side, and planted with a mixture of rambling roses in various shades of the same colour.

In a fit of economy we had decided to make the top of the wall, capitals and balls in cement. Wooden mouldings were made for the capitals and that was simple. Mr Paccini, in his ingenious way, resolved the question of the mould for the balls by using a half sphere and then sealing the two halves together. It is getting the size and proportions right that is difficult, and now I was faced with the problem again.

The entrance to a property is fundamental; it gives the

introduction you wish to impart from the outside. I had driven all over the outskirts and countryside of Florence taking photographs of possibilities and details. It was like a jigsaw puzzle, a piece here and there to make up a finished picture. First of all, the entrance had to be off the road, so cars waiting for the gates to open didn't obstruct the traffic. I decided on a half-moon shape for this and to follow the curve either side with a sloping wall, finishing either end with a column, one tall to hold the gates and the other small as a finial. But they must both carry the obligatory ball. I had used the original mould of a 50-centimetre diameter and on the small column it looked right. On the big one it looked wrong. The young man was getting tired. I just hoped he wouldn't lose his balance. I tried to decide quickly, walking back and looking from the road then from the side. The young man said he was getting cramp. I asked him if he could stand up for a minute. It was when he did, that I realised what was wrong – perspective. We made the balls bigger in diameter by 20 centimetres and everything fell into place. Voilà! From the stables to the entrance gate it was 700 metres, a good morning's run or trot. We had moved the horses up to the top of the drive, making good-sized fields either side with train sleepers. I loved the strong, sturdy look of them and the fact that they were tarred, for then horses wouldn't chew on them. Tar is also dark brown, not black, and for a country place I preferred it. Having planted cypress trees and yew bushes clipped to balls (again – it must be one of my fixations) along the side of the driveway I was now ready for the gates.

While scouting around Florence and the immediate vicinity, I had found the exact gates I would like to copy, or nearly, in Via Bolognese. Just by the bridge over the torrent in San Giustino there are two brothers who run a forge,

Angelo and Massimo. Very early one morning while the mist was still blanketing the sleeping valleys of the Valdarno, we set off, Angelo and I, for Florence. We arrived in Via Bolognese as the sun slipped over the *cupola* of the *duomo*, making the rooftops glisten with golden dew. The echo of carts as they cleaned the silent street seemed alien in such antiquity. I showed Angelo the gates. 'I need to get a close look at those finials, Signora, a photo won't do it and for that we will need a ladder.' He looked resigned to another wasted morning. Like a magician I pulled a rolled-up ladder from the back of the car, an estate car! Up he went and started to make a sketch and take measurements. Suddenly a yellow light started to flash on the side. I grabbed the ladder, 'Quick Angelo, *scendi*!'[1] He jumped down. I motioned for him to grab the other end of the ladder and started walking down the street, and Angelo had to follow, being attached to the other end.

On the way home he was silent, pensive. 'Signora, can I ask you something?' I nodded and smiled. 'Did you have permission to copy those gates?', – 'No,' I told him. 'It wasn't a private house with one person to ask.' That said it all. In Italy bureaucracy can bury you before you can even start.

Getting permission to renovate, especially old buildings, is difficult in any country, but I had the *architetto*. He knew everyone. The Borro estate is part of four councils, Terranuova Bracciolini and Loro Ciuffenna, which are the main ones, and then there are two smaller parts in Castiglion Fibocchi and Laterina. I gradually got to know everyone. I'm not one to beat about the bush; I get straight to the point. I

1. get down

45

had to learn to temper my methods. Carlo Pasquine is the mayor of Terranuova, and has a brilliant mind. He was a professor of history, and once he launches into his favourite subject there is no stopping him. Soon after we arrived, he invited himself and a group of his councillors to dinner at Number 4. I was nervous; what do I give them? Will it be all right to eat in the kitchen? I had wonderful Beppina, an ace up my sleeve. Beppina was my lifesaver. She lived in the village with her husband who, having been made redundant because of an accident at work, I would meet occasionally in the bar, where the men would sit making their drinks last as long as possible while watching sport on the TV and reading sporting newspapers, especially concerning cycling – a major passion in this area. They had two adult children and she would come to work on her old, rickety bicycle, never having learned to drive. She was exceptionally tall compared to the average and teutonic in build. We would sit together and discuss diets, hair dyes and just life in general over a cup of coffee, not much different from the men in the bar! It took a long time to persuade Beppina to sit with me at the kitchen table. 'I have too much to do to sit and gossip,' she would say. She stripped the beds every day and hung the blankets and sheets out of the windows to air, summer and winter, beating the cushions with a bamboo beater. The floors shone with polish. We had used wooden floors in plain planks of Russian larch in the bedrooms and they became mellow and a deep rich brown over the months as Beppina's care brought them back to life.

Beppina's mission in life, however, is cooking. A master of making real country food, she would make the simplest ingredients into dishes you would dream about. In the summer we planted pots of every type of herb available, dried them in the autumn and chopped and stored them in airtight bottles for winter use. She would make the tastiest stews of rabbit marinated in milk and chopped bay leaves; wild boar in red wine and blackcurrant juice with herbs such as rosemary, sage and peppercorns and slices of red onion; chicken breast beaten until it was almost transparent and then left for three hours in olive oil, balsamic vinegar and a teaspoon of honey. She made sauces and juices to make your mouth water; meat loaf made with a mixture of the leftovers and served with mashed potatoes and thick, creamy gravy. She is famous for her rich, spicy tomato sauce. In fact when we started our product line, it was one of the first things to be bottled and sold in the shop 'Il Borro a Casa'. That night we had spicy bean soup with rosemary, and roast pork with mushrooms in white wine. We gave them a simple but robust local Chianti.

We were all a bit stiff and staid to begin with, rigid smiles and handshakes. '*Buona sera, buona sera.*' Hands were rubbed together although it was hardly cold. We had to sit down directly at table. The only other option being the church pew. Carlo, the Mayor, has travelled widely and disappears regularly, heading in the direction of the Himalayas or China and he loves to talk about his trips. His stories are fascinating and enthralling. Some of his friends had obviously heard them before, there was nudging, winking, rolling of eyes, and we all started to relax. The wine flowed, the fire glowed, and faces became pink and eyes shone. Voices gradually became louder. Beppina gave me the thumbs up sign. We finished the evening on a first name basis and I really felt I had made friends with my neighbours. One of the reasons for this impromptu meeting, apart from getting to know each other, was to enquire about the Terranuova autumn fair. 'Would we take a stand?' I immediately said yes, and this was the first of a long series of events we organised over the next few years. Not only with Terranuova but with the other councils too. Sometimes we had luncheons or dinners attended by all four mayors. Seeing them sitting at the same table engrossed in animated but friendly conversation was a great satisfaction.

Whenever I think of politics, which is not often, I shy away like a nervous horse. There is an invisible sign with 'Keep Out, Private Property, Top Secret', etched on the subject, but not 'War Zone'. Yes, there is bickering, name-calling, squabbles galore but this is normal and it doesn't stop when the elections or referendums are over. It is the natural continuous state of affairs, the norm. What I find truly admirable about the Italians is that in the end it makes no permanent difference to them who is in government. Yet be careful, it is a very serious business, not to be taken lightly. They will look at you from the greatest height they can achieve and think, if not say, 'Only a foreigner could ask such an indelicate question.' You never ask, 'Who did you vote for?' It is the biggest gaffe you can make and you will immediately be put in your place.

Once, long ago, when I had been married about a year, we went up the incredibly narrow, twisting road to Fiesole to vote. We always did things at the last minute, no time should ever be lost on trivialities like traffic or parking, slow coaches can be passed on the inside and pavements are as good a place as any to park on, and, in any case, how long can it take to vote? We arrived at 10.25 p.m. on Sunday night.

We rushed up the elementary school steps, warmed on either side by yellow suns with smiling faces, bobbing sailing boats with tiny sails, in seas of an impossible blue, inhabited by fish twice the size of a submarine. Is it wisdom or innocence from virgin brains? No time to contemplate, on, on into a classroom of formica and steel. We were presented with voting forms and asked to wait until our names were called and then were given three forms folded in on themselves three times, in pastel shades of green, pink and yellow. We were, in fact, the last and didn't have to wait in the usual queue. In the corridors people were standing about chatting, smoking, looking tired and bored. 'Ciao, see you tomorrow'; it was the end of a long day.

There were two booths on either side of the room behind the officiating desk. Ferruccio went into one and I, a few moments later, into the other. Pencils were tethered to a wooden board. The pink form was obvious, I made my cross and deliberately folded it in three again, the same with the pale green form, but the yellow form had me stumped. Ferruccio had explained to me very carefully what I had to do, where to put my cross and how, but now with all the rushing, my mind was a blank. 'Damn!' I peeked out from behind the curtain. There he was leaning up against the wall, the sole of one shoe resting against the plaster. I remember thinking he would leave a mark. 'Pssssst.' He didn't hear. I took a few steps forward, 'The yellow one, where?' I spread my hands in an interrogative gesture. Pandemonium struck, voices were raised, my arm was roughly taken. '*Signora, Signora, invalido, invalido. Il voto é invalido.*'[1] I was heavily pregnant with twins so I think they took pity on my obviously disturbed mental state. Did I not understand the gravity of the situation? By now I most certainly did, and went home clutching my tummy and looking properly chastised.

1. The vote is invalid

One warm winter's day, I took advantage of the clement weather to take the children to the zoo in Pistoia. The boys and Vivia were small, about five and three. As we came off the *autostrade* I could find no indication for the zoo. The traffic was thick, and at one point we were nose to tail going into Pistoia centre. Walking between the cars was a man selling *l'Unita*, the communist newspaper. I had my window open and he offered it to me, 'No thank you, I am *Demo-cristiano*, but I wonder if you could tell me the way to the zoo?'

'You are going in the wrong direction, Signora. You should have turned left off the *autostrada*, in fact Signora, you should go left altogether.'

It didn't click for a moment what he meant and then I started to laugh. He stopped the traffic with a flourish, enabling me to make an illegal U-turn. Smiling, we waved our thanks. That is the way I naively envisage politics and religion. Wouldn't it be so civilized if we could live with our differences with humour and friendship without feeling we have to force our opinions down other people's throats? Unfortunately, that's just a pipe dream.

Actually, the day turned into one of those you don't forget. There were hardly any other people, because it was a weekday in the winter. The children were allowed to play with a chimpanzee. He accompanied us back to the car. The children wanted to take him home. 'We have enough monkeys at home as it is,' I said. We took a photo with it instead. All four of them sitting on the curb by the car park. I still have it – a happy memory of a happy day.

I have always felt that the main problem with politics is too vast a choice, it's confusing. A real case of too many Chiefs and no Indians. If a government is made up of a coalition of incompatible parties, how can it govern? I feel it could be compared more realistically with an elaborate game of musical chairs; the chairs themselves have gold gilt legs, carved backs, and are upholstered in silk brocade. When the music stops, someone will be left standing. But then the music will start again and it will be someone else's turn to stand out. I have had it explained to me many times. The politics of Italy and its constitution today are the consequences of its history. From the dictatorship of Mussolini and fascism there was a hard swing in the opposite direction. The pendulum swung towards communism, Italian style, and socialism. Two extremes, but with so many people putting their oar in, there has never been any great fear of dictatorship again, in any form. The Italian, as I know him, and after all I have five half-Italians as my children, are not easy to govern. They are too individual. I notice that a man is a Bolognese, Romano, Milanese before calling himself Italian.

This again is reminiscent of a time when Italy was divided into 26 kingdoms or dukedoms. However, there has been a gradual change in this respect. 'Laws that apply to others do not apply to me personally,' I think is the general feeling in Italy. Everyone is a law unto himself. I have no right to pass judgement but I will give you two trivial examples that, when they occured, left me feeling hopeless.

One side of my house is skirted by a wall and ramp leading up to the main gate. On this wall I have planted climbing roses in bright apricot. They flower in spring and autumn, are cared for, dead-headed and clipped back, growing directly below my bedroom window.

One spring morning I heard a clipping sound through my open window. Looking out I found a lady with a basket and secateurs denuding my wall of its treasured roses. This was no crime of passion but well calculated. I quickly went out and politely said '*Buongiorno.*' There was no reply, and she can't have been more than two metres away from me. I repeated, '*Buongiorno, mi scusi ma quelli sono i miei rosi.*'[1]

She didn't reply until she had taken the last rose.

'They're on the road, and if you don't like it call the *carabinieri.*'

If you think about this mean incident rationally, it is understandable. She probably lived in an apartment in the middle of many apartment blocks in a sea of cement. Not a blade of grass to be seen. She drives past a house obviously blessed with a big garden and thinks, 'What are a few roses to them?' She is right! It's the attitude towards private property that's wrong. All she had to do was ask.

On the other hand, there is no 'road rage', not as it is known in England. The flagrant cutting in and disregard for fellow motorists is rampant in Italy. You can wait in an ever-increasing traffic jam, desperately trying to get children to school, while your neighbours chat to each other through car windows. In England pistols would be drawn and blood spilled long before there had been any build up in the traffic. Here horns will blow, rude gestures will be made but it's all part of the hurly-burly of life. No big deal!

1. Good day, excuse me but those are my roses

6 Wild Boar and Riding Accidents

In the main courtyard there is a group of holm-oaks. They must have been there long before anything else, when the land was wild and inhabited only by wolves and wild boar. The wolves of the Pratomagno were legendary, the only predators of the wild boar. Today they are being reintroduced. Today, the wild boar damages and destroys whole fields of corn. Nature will have her balance and the government will pay for any stray sheep that get eaten as an aperitif on the way to the main course.

There are many tall stories told about boar. Stefano, the gamekeeper, once told me that they could jump 120 centimetres high. I nodded and looked properly impressed all the time, thinking, 'He really means 60 centimetres, the height of a washing machine.' It's difficult to get a pony to jump 60 centimetres, let alone a pig.

That winter Ferruccio planted an experimental field of American sweetcorn. He fenced it off protectively. It was watered and nurtured in every way and grew to very satisfactory proportions. One morning there were sombre faces and shaking heads in the main courtyard. The field had been completely demolished, flattened overnight. Wild boar had jumped the fence – and that is not a fisherman's tale, I saw the results myself!

I had never actually seen a wild boar up close until we were invited to a boar hunt in Maremma. The morning was uneventful, we stood around and waited; we could hear shots and shouts in the distance but nothing came our way. At midday we climbed down from our hide. Basically, it was a platform built in a tree with a ladder extending from it to the ground. We made our way back to the farmhouse. Under the fruit trees at the back, long trestle tables had been laid out. Open fires burned and sausages and steaks were spitting on the grills. Big bowls of pasta steamed. My stomach rumbled. I hadn't really taken any hard exercise but the smells of cooking were making my mouth water. It was still warm and I was passed a glass of cool white wine. Delicious! I had only taken a sip when I heard my hostess call, 'Mandy, you know how to ride don't you?'

'Yessss.'

'Could you please go with the others to bring the boar down as one man is sick today and I have an extra horse.'

My stomach lurched; I took a gulp of my wine. 'Okay.' I simply couldn't lose face, I would look so silly if I said I was afraid and I hadn't been quick enough to make a plausible excuse. Now I had to go through with it. I knew those Maremmano horses, they were a bit like the Andalusian, with long manes and tails and proud, fierce heads, yet bigger and sturdier. They were bred for use as a *buttero's* horse – for the Maremmano cowboy.

My new means of transport was equipped with the regulatory American saddle, armchair-like with a high back and huge pommel. Well, he wasn't going to stand still and let this strange person on his back. I was given a strong foot-up and nearly flew over the other side but, grabbing the pommel, we set off up the hill after the others. I gradually settled in and looked around me. Up here the trees were scarce, the ground yellow, hard and dry, cracking into deep furrows running down the hillside. The vegetation was mostly low scrub with gorse, heather, rosemary and a few stunted oaks. The air was balmy with a maritime feel to it.

As we climbed higher the countryside spread out below us. It was mostly flat, neatly trimmed and patterned into fields of corn and groves of fruit and olives. In the far distance, the blue haze of the sea evaporated into the sky. I began to relax and enjoy myself. My horse seemed to have come to the conclusion that I was there to stay, for the immediate future at least, and plodded along in a bored and resigned fashion behind the others in Indian file. Up ahead there was a mounted *buttero* guarding a line-up of corpses – boar. Most of them lay on their backs with the soft under-stomach exposed, as pink as a baby's. Mouths hung open and black eyes which would never blink again stared as a fly buzzed by and settled. Their snouts were long with the little rounded point you often see quiver as a domestic pig snuffles the air. Their stained and yellow tusks, a dentist's nightmare, were what made the difference, while their hoof-topped legs – far too dainty to carry their weight – stuck rigidly in the air.

The next part of this little adventure had been worrying me slightly. Horses don't like pigs, especially their smell, and they also hate the smell of blood. My new friend was going to have to carry a profusely bleeding pig down a ripped, slippery hill. But most important of all, I was going to be part of the cargo too and, as yet, not a dead weight! I could only use one hand to guide the horse while the other clutched the boar. My fingers clung to his thick, wiry black hair. It was just like a brush, totally unbendable. Blood ran down the horse's legs in rivulets as he negotiated his way down, taking tiny steps first one way, then the other. I was simply a passenger. This was his job and he didn't need any interference from me. Years later I was putting up a mounted boar's head in the hunting dining room. On a little brass plaque was written the date and the weight – 146 kilograms. That horse was carrying more than 200 kilograms, mostly on his shoulders, down a slippery, crumbling hill.

We all ride to one extent or another. Salvatore played polo occasionally. Jamie rode for exercise with friends on week-ends once the shooting season was over. Vivia was the same; but Olly and Vicky took it seriously. Two of the polo ponies went back to England. The total lack of discipline, plus the wonders of country life had gone completely to their heads. It became a major feat to catch them, we spent hours working out strategies – even starvation didn't work. They could see us coming a mile away and definitely had our number. The final straw was a spectacular rodeo that put Salvatore into Arezzo hospital for a week. As he went in one door, our Australian nanny came out of another and gave me her notice in no uncertain terms. She had received a well-aimed kick on the bottom. I must admit I felt like giving her one on the other side, just to even things out. She had spent four days complaining in a loud voice about the Italian hospital system, not realising the more rumpus she caused the worse it would get.

From then on the riding saga was in full swing. We bought horses and sent them back on a regular basis. Finally, both Olly and Vicky seemed to find the right combination. I cannot remember the name of Olly's final choice; we had been through so many, I just called them 'Cicco' or 'Cicca' rather than 'Darling'. Vicky's horse we called Ginger Snap. She was a large gangly chestnut mare, very young with no concentration at all. She seemed to be looking everywhere except where she was going. When jumping this can be a bit off-putting, but

56

Vicky loved her. Why didn't I learn from my mistakes? I did buy them body-protectors, especially imported from England, but the difficulty was in getting them to wear them.

Vicky was eleven that summer. Both she and Olly were now really into the jumping scene, going to competitions most weekends. Their horses were groomed till they shone with domino patterns carefully marked on their rumps, manes and tails plaited, hooves oiled, and tack polished till it gleamed. I just wished they would take as much trouble with their own appearance, but you can't have everything.

Preparing for jumping events takes practise and one morning in June jumps had been set up for this purpose. Luckily I was at home that morning when I heard a young voice calling me from the gates, 'Mandy, Mandy, Vicky has fallen off.' I pressed the button to open the gates; nothing happened. I tried the light on the stairs, the same. The child at the gate was crying, 'She can't get up.' We were locked in and the only way to get out was through the villa onto the back road. I started running. I grabbed a workman and his little red Panda. His name was Marcello, an older man, sensible and kind, my first piece of luck, and he didn't hesitate. Driving across the bumpy, dry fields we finally got to her. As illogical as children can be, her first words were about her back-protector. She wasn't wearing it. I hesitated to move her, but I didn't see much option. I had no phone, no idea how long an ambulance would take to get there. And she had already tried to get up, so the damage, if any, was already done. The drive to Arezzo hospital took an age, Vicky silently weeping. Marcello and I tried to encourage her, 'It'll be all right, don't worry, it won't be anything serious.' But it was. Vicky had broken and displaced both pelvic bones on one side, cracked both sides of her sacroiliac and damaged a muscle in her back.

We were back in Arezzo hospital. She was encased in plaster from the top of the thigh to under the breastbone for one month, and kept permanently still in bed. We obtained a special hospital bed that we could lever up and down. That summer we lived in Number 4 with the shutters closed against the heat, and with no real regard for time. In fact we almost totally inverted day and night. In the cool hours of the night we would open the windows and create currents of delicious cool air, real air, not from the fan. Full of the scents and sounds of summer nights. The crickets stopped and started as if a switch had been thrown. We began to be able to tell the time by them – 10.30 p.m. was definitely when the night shift clocked off and 3.30 p.m. when the afternoon shift came on.

The scent from Angela's garden wafted up on the breeze seeming far stronger in the dark. Once the watering system started at 3.00 a.m., the currents of air cooled. There were no horses in the boxes but the clanking of buckets for their feed meant it was 5.00 a.m. and shortly after we would hear the buggy start up. All work is done either very early in the morning or late in the afternoon in the summer to avoid the heat. We watched endless videos, read books and just chatted for hours on end. The day was spent sleeping on and off, and cooling Vicky with sponge baths. We put sweet-scented ice towels on her forehead and she would fall back to sleep again. There was endless dowsing with talcum powder to help the itching and exploratory invasions of a knitting needle. I caught up on the mountain of paperwork that had been on my conscience for ages: letters written after months of delay, bills finally paid, accounts rendered, and so we came to the end of the month. Two weeks in a wheel-chair, two weeks on crutches, and back on the same horse over the same jump – this time with a body-protector.

* * *

A naughty niece of mine came to stay. She finished up in hospital with an injured knee. Were we accident-prone or just careless? My turn came sometime later. I loved riding out with Bonnie on Woody, the only pony remaining from the original three. On that day she decided it was time for a break and would not be caught so Brandy was saddled and waiting for me when I got down to the yard. I didn't like Brandy and Bonnie liked her even less, so she followed at a respectful distance. After a trying half-hour with Brandy doing her usual jitterbug, ready to take flight at the smallest piece of paper or bird in a bush, I decided to make for home the shortest way possible – down the road. Big mistake! A huge lorry transporting gas came along the road towards us. There was no way to avoid it. On both sides of the road large trenches had been dug, wide and deep to drain the water from the fields. I flagged the lorry down and kindly he came to a complete stop. I coaxed Brandy on with kind words of encouragement, kicked her and swore at her to no avail. Here in front of her was a monster, a dragon out to get her at all costs. She continued to back towards the ditch, eyes staring, nostrils flared, her concentration riveted on the lorry. We fell backwards into the ditch. As she came backwards on top of me, I put my arm out to protect my head and I heard a dull pop from my wrist. There was no pain, just rage which enveloped me as I scrambled on hands and knees into the freshly ploughed field above me. Needless to say both the lorry and Brandy cleared off as fast as they could, down the road in opposite directions. I got to my feet and clambered down to the road covered in mud. What was that terrible smell? Not mud, it was manure! The field had just been fertilised. We had had rain the night before and it had softened and spread widely.

'Damn, damn, damn.' I stank like a sewer rat. It was in my boots, hair, everywhere. Another lorry came into sight, this time one I knew, Mr Mattessoni bringing us plants. I climbed in regardless.

'Chanel No. 5 I presume?'

'No Mr Mattessoni, No. 2 Mixed Manure.'

Salvatore insisted on taking me immediately for an X-ray. He seemed immune to my new heavy scent. I gave in but insisted on going to Montevarchi, not Arezzo. 'Please Salva, I couldn't bear to see that doctor again, he will think we are completely incompetent.' I had to stay in the waiting room for some time. I didn't sit down but stood with Salva as far from the other patients as possible. There were a lot of curious stares and wrinkled noses but finally it was my turn. In the X-ray room all was ready, only the doctor was missing. The door opened and there he was, the doctor from Arezzo! I stared at him. This is some kind of hallucination, it can't be. 'Good morning Mrs Ferragamo.'

Rather rudely but understandably in the situation, I said, 'What are you doing here?'

'Oh, I've just been transferred from Arezzo and it's my first day. Now what have we here?'

I wanted to say nothing at all, or, 'I was just in the area and thought I'd drop in.' But there was nothing for it; I had to hand over my wrist.

There is one member of the family I have not mentioned with regard to horses, my husband Ferruccio. He doesn't really like them, nor trust them, and considering the history I have just recorded you can hardly blame him. 'Not reliable, nice to look at from afar.' That was until he fell in love at Verona Fair. We went to the Verona Horse Fair looking for molasses. It was the new fad for a healthy horse and our horses were spoilt if indisciplined. Four of us set out, Olivia, Vicky, Ferruccio and I. It was November but the weather was still clement, if not spring-like. We spent a pleasant day watching western riding, show-jumping and the Andalusians doing their circus tricks. There was every type of stand selling everything from wood shavings to insurance. Around 4 p.m. we started toward the car in the hope of beating the traffic, laden down with large canisters of molasses. We were nearly at the car park when lightning struck. Standing right in our path was the most beautiful Andalusian mare.

Totally black, her coat reflected the last rays of sun. She had perfect proportions and such a pretty face; large soft eyes in a small expressive head, unlike the usual Andalusian with its Roman nose. Her ears were pricked and she had no fear of being petted and touched by all and sundry. Two large red rosettes either side of the bridle made her black coat seem even deeper in colour, if that were possible. Her mane was thick and luxurious, falling half way down her neck, and her tail touched the ground. She was a real beauty. Like a film star receiving her due.

Ferruccio put down his load and reached out to her tentatively. Bang! he was a goner. We went back into the throngs of people and half an hour later she was ours. There was great excitement in the car on the way home, now in the worst traffic. 'When will she arrive, what will we call her?' Olly came up with a great name – Pan di Spagna. It was perfect, being a soft sweet sponge cake, much loved by Italians.

Pandi, as she soon became known, is essentially a brood mare. We thought looking for a worthy mate for such a star would not be easy, but it was, and we found him in the most obvious place, on TV. Attila was an actor. It is superfluous to say that no horse has been so petted and cared for. Their foal Forest arrived at 5 a.m. on a cold winter morning, black like his mother but with white socks. Pandi was by nature a good mother and within 20 minutes of his birth, the girls were touching and stroking his damp curly coat. He staggered on stilt-like legs, little tail wagging, nuzzling and butting his mother as he sucked at her milk, while she placidly munched on hay and the girls sat in the straw a few steps away.

Life is cruel and at five months Forest needed to be weaned; being a growing colt he could not simply go in with the other horses, and he needed a friend, so Pinocchio came into our lives. He was a baby donkey the same age as Forest. His huge ears lay flat along his neck; his liquid eyes searched while his little muzzle sniffed the air for any scent of his mother. He was a minute donkey, brown all over with a white muzzle and chest. His great ears were defined with a black line. Pandi hated him. Mother having been removed, Forest and Pinocchio moved in together and for the next three years they were never further apart than a few feet. On one occasion Forest, full name Black Forest, as in cake, had to go to Bologna for a little operation. On arrival the surgeon came out to greet us already in his green garb. The back of the van gradually opened and there stood the strange couple, staring down at him. 'What is that?'

'That is his friend and he won't go anywhere without him.'

Once the second set of gates were mounted and shut, the yard was finished. These gates were a copy of the entrance gate, smaller and without the sloping walls. They closed the yard at the level of the *tinaia* giving plenty of space to manoeuvre. The whole area adjacent to the stables, cellar and *tinaia* was paved with *pietra serena*, ridged in the usual

62

herringbone fashion, used for centuries. Unfortunately, it was not done by hand, as that would be impossible today for such a large area. This ridging was ideal to avoid horses and people slipping on the incline down to the cellar.

I made a tack room out of an area which is nestled between the cellar and the stables. There was no roof left but it was high enough for me to put in a hanging loft reached by a wooden ladder-like stair. The floor, like the stables, was laid with terracotta tiles of the old type, again used for centuries in gardens and stables, deep and narrow, about 20 centimetres by five centimetres and laid in a herringbone pattern. They take a lot of wear and resist the hard chemicals used to keep a place of this kind hygienic. A central drainage system ran down the centre aisle and all the boxes had an imperceptible gradient to make this functional. The four boxes were large, made with wooden partitions to a specific height and with metal railings above. Each box had a window and, naturally, opened onto the central aisle.

The tack room was done in the same manner. In the tack room we kept, apart from all the saddlery and horse food, everything necessary for the dogs, including a full-sized bath. It was waist-height which meant giving a dog a bath was a pleasure with no heaving in and out and no bad back at the end of it. We also had a wall dryer at the same level, very professional. The dogs hated it and entered the tack room with mixed feelings – food on the one hand, bath on the other. There was also a central stove for drying in the winter and finally a large table for cleaning tack and drinking coffee. It was a warm cosy place in the winter with the cassette player blearing out disco music, horses' heads thrust out of windows and mouthfuls of feed being chewed in an almost rhythmic fashion. I had made three kennels in the manner of pigsties with a closed-off inner area. These closed the circle formed by the main utility area of cellar, stables, tack room and *tinaia*.

The driveway lead through on the valley side, and we skirted it with a verge of grass and cypress trees, but without the yew balls. I needed to build a retaining wall. The land slipped rapidly away here to the river valley below the Borro village. We managed this by injecting pylons of armoured cement, integrated with wire mesh containers filled with heavy stones. In all, once finished, it gave a pleasing effect with a low finishing wall in stone curving and running down the side of the *limonaia* to the back entrance to the Italian garden.

Once I'd attacked both these projects, this area was complete, except for the villa.

7 The *Granaio* and the Swimming Pool

Looking from the terrace towards the Borro, my eye was drawn towards the area below the villa. There were chickens scattered here and there; dogs in kennels; rabbits in hutches and a few fruit trees. The ground was uneven and sloped down in terraces towards a tumble-down wall and what seemed to be a few rotten wooden posts and metal hoops; perhaps the remains of a covered walkway. I felt sorry for the dogs and turning to Bonnie said, 'We had better get them new lodgings, find them good homes because, in any case, this I will make into an Italian garden.'

I was surprised, I hadn't consciously formed this idea but now it was quite clear in my mind's eye. I always carry paper and pencil with me, so I started to draw then and there. My busy fingers started to sketch almost spontaneously, what I could see and what I was picturing. I could almost smell the box and the roses, hear the water falling in the fountain. Nothing in the building or creative world I was dealing with could be separated from its surrounds. Ideas always multiply, feeding off each other and dividing as the creation of life itself. The garden was clear in my mind's eye; it was enclosed on two sides by buildings. I was now going to synchronize all these parts.

Down one side and part of the front of the garden there is

a long L-shaped building. It had originally been used as a *granaio*[1] where the grain was dried and stored. It consisted of three floors with a central flight of wide stairs, with an open terrace which looked towards the Borro on the top floor. It is important to me, vital I would say, to walk around, to spend time allowing a building to talk to me and get into my head. Then I can see how it can be developed and adapted to my needs and I can imagine people living in these creations. This is a luxury few people in the decorating and renovating world can afford or be afforded. Difficult to explain, you have to be there or that way inclined.

We decided to make the top floor of the *granaio* into the hunting dining room. The terrace was an extra, plus a perfect place to have an aperitif and point out places of interest to guests. It gave you a complete picture of the entire garden, indispensable to me while designing. We opened up the windows that certainly must have been there originally. The floor had to be reconstructed but I saved the old terracotta tiles, had them sand-blasted, and replaced them exactly as they had been before. The skirting board and ceiling cornice we had made of wood. Along the cornice at regular intervals I placed a diamond-shaped piece of wood painted green. Little iron wall-brackets were painted green also. The central light was the *pièce de résistance*. In London I found a workshop that specialises in furniture and accessories made of antlers. Red Mile made me a gigantic chandelier of deer's antlers. It was the focal point. With boars' heads mounted on wooden plaques along the walls, the hunting theme was very evident. We made a pizza oven and a high open fire.

One major problem held us back, a central pillar. The roof would not have the necessary support if we removed it, but

1. granary

leaving it would reduce the dimensions of the room. Ferruccio insisted it go, and in fact he came up with the solution. A tension bar was hooked and cemented into the wall either side of the roof with a central screw to tighten it. Pressure was applied until the required support was achieved. The whole bar was then sunk into the central beam where it wasn't visible. It was now a good-sized room. We could fit 50 to 60 people sitting at long trestle tables. I made green tablecloths, with arrangements of autumn leaves and chestnuts. It became a jolly, warm place to be. We used it for many events, conferences, exhibitions and parties of all kinds.

I never knew what they used the terrace for originally; with its very low wall it was dangerous. I heightened the wall to 40 centimetres and put a simple iron railing all around, leaving enough room to use the wall as a seat. A small pergola at one end was covered in creeper vines, and red and white grapes crept up the wall to the railing at the other end. We used this area often for barbeques and on a summer evening it was magical. The lights in the medieval village cast shadows on the old stone streets, lighting up steps and arches here and there. The fountain played in the garden below and a welcome cool breeze kept us company while we sipped a glass of iced white wine.

Adjacent to the dining room, up a couple of stairs on the short leg of the 'L', I built a kitchen, two bathrooms and a bedroom. These are useful when catering for large numbers. I divided the kitchen into two with a large table in the middle so cooking lessons could be arranged.

The floor below was of exactly the same dimensions with the terrace incorporated into the whole, and I gave this room the same floor treatment, but did little else, apart from the windows. This room became partly Salvatore's office and partly a storage room. It was good for this purpose, being close to a double-door exit on the landing. It must have been used originally for bringing in sacks of corn. It also meant that the furniture didn't have to negotiate the stairs. We had thought at one point of using this area for antique restoration, and giving lessons but in the end it never happened. On the courtyard side of the short side of the 'L' we made a hunting office and a long changing room with our usual airing cupboards for wet clothes, gun racks and metal lockers with special locks for whoever wished to leave a gun overnight. The ground floor on the garden side of the long leg was simply made into a *limonaia*, and here the garden and terraces have the biggest impact.

In Italy, summer really starts in earnest in June and continues through to September. There are exceptions, of course, but when planning the construction of a swimming pool it's better to be the devil's advocate. There are many months when it is very cold in this region, with snow and ice. Arctic winds blow over the snow-capped peaks of the Pratomagno. An indoor pool would be such a luxury. Think of winter outside and the tropics inside. Coming in stiff and cold from a day's shooting and then wallowing in warm water. Swimming is the best exercise for stiff muscles and sore backs. In the summer with French doors leading onto a terrace, it would be almost outside, and there would be no need for all the cleaning an outside pool requires. And so it went on in my mind, round and round, weighing the pros and cons, but the final decision was made for me when I walked into the long, narrow cellar that almost met the villa (and would later). It was perfect for a pool. Now I had some real fun.

Building the swimming pool was a decorator's delight. It

had vaulted ceilings and three recessed windows looking over the future garden, and my imaginary terraces, where we would, eventually, sunbathe. Here there were no restrictions on me as far as tradition was concerned. A swimming pool, partially underground, needs special wall and floor treatment even with continuous air-conditioning, at massive expense. Condensation would cause havoc with any ordinary paint and plaster. Stone would be good, so would marble, but too expensive for such a big area. This is when I met another character I will never forget, Emilio.

He is a painter, come everything. Small, with a head of curly white hair, a charming cheeky smile and a very infectious laugh. He is also a genius. The pointed vaults with their elegant sweeping curves made me want to add pillars. Pillars made me think of harems and Roman baths. That's what I wanted – pillars disappearing into the water. I won't go into all the details, they are long and laborious, but that's what we made – a Roman bath, a bit kitsch but fun. Emilio solved the problem of wall treatment by mixing marble dust and stucco, forming them into slabs to match the floor, which we had laid with untreated Italian limestone. We enlarged the area as far as we could on either side, making the windows into large arches with glass doors leading onto the terrace. I bought Roman brackets in, of all places, New York; Roman friezes in London; and Angelo the blacksmith made me Roman-style wrought-iron seats with curved arms. It was a project I really enjoyed and especially with Emilio's ever-present sense of humour. He made his laboratory in the ruins of the villa, where he and his crew would sit around a brazier eating their lunch.

One day they found a kitten just a few days old and Emilio adopted it. I asked him what he had called it. There was sniggering all round and Emilio's cheeky grin appeared.

'Puccinella,' he said. I found out later that he had called it Mandy after me. I wonder if it had anything to do with the old saying: 'When the cat's away the mice will play'? We made saunas and showers and joined the swimming pool area to the villa with a flight of steps leading into a gym. I eventually turned the room across the corridor into a billiard room so all the playthings were together. Billiards to gym to sauna to swimming pool, finishing up in the *Casa di Caccia*,[1] all surrounding the garden – my Italian garden.

1. Shooting lodge

8 The Italian Garden

We were driving around, looking for a fountain, or someone to make us one, and getting there at an average speed of 100 miles an hour, but then this was normal. Driving fast is a national trait in Italy and as much part of being a man and as macho as having the equipment to prove it. Driving up behind an unsuspecting tourist with lights flashing as if you are going to ram him is all par for the course. The tourist will bolt for the inside lane like a frightened hare, angry horns blare and we fly past while I wave and mouth apologies.

As work on the swimming pool drew to a close, I had turned my mind to the garden. There was not one geometrically correct line anywhere; everything was out of sync and off kilter. First I tackled the terrace, intending it to have three purposes. One was for eating out, so it had to adjoin the villa, two for sunbathing, so it also had to run off the swimming area and, last but not least, it had to lead on to the *limonaia*. This produced a problem of heights, as each area was at a different level. I had to follow the lowest, obviously. Luckily it was the *limonaia*. To move large plants in pots needs equipment which is easier to use without steps. I also needed double glass doors leading from the *limonaia* on to the terrace. The terrace was not all the same width, it couldn't be. The line that had to be straight was where the terrace defined the garden, enabling me to design geometrical patterns. The far end of the terrace in front of the villa was wider than the swimming pool end, useful to place a large table in order to dine al fresco; the narrowest part being the short leg down the side of the *limonaia*.

Now for the garden itself. This area had to be flat. Taking the lowest point at the old wall, looking over the Borro, we removed all the earth, right up to the terrace, making a supporting wall of about two metres. On studying my new flat area from the *caccia* terrace, I could see it was still lop-sided. Heightening the old stone wall all the way around the garden, I reinstated the covered walkway, which ran parallel to it. I planted wisteria in the usual lilac-blue colour along the wall, except in one corner, where I put a patch of white to break monotony. Still the garden was lop-sided. I needed to chop off a lump at the villa end – but how? Back to the terrace to gaze and think. I knew what I wanted. I had seen it in my mind on that first day; but how to accomplish it. I finally returned to the age-old solution of a yew hedge, leaving a wedge of garden, where we planted six holm-oaks to protect us from the houses across the road, and to give shade for a camellia garden. A stone path twisted through it, following on from the walkway, which became a naturally hidden area quite spontaneously. Here I planted camellia of different types, but always in white. When I can, I like to use white as it shows up at night. Finally, I could square out the remaining area. Now it was simply mathematical, made graceful with sweeping curves and circles all fitting into each other in a natural and sinuous way, one movement flowing effortlessly into the next.

Once I found the centre point of the garden we took this in a direct line to the terrace wall. Here curving steps would embrace a wall fountain with its basin full of ninfea. I would have three founts of water, a small wall bowl with a tap and decorative back making a break between swimming pool and main house, one between the steps down to the garden and, lastly, the main fountain in the centre; each one pumping water to the next in a continual circle. It should work, and it did. This main one was the fountain we were now on our way to look for, once more at Verona Fair. I had looked at various fountains in Florence and around the area, and had found exactly what I wanted but at an awful expense. I loved the idea of shells in three layers getting larger as they descended. The shape of the rounded outside of a shell is pleasing and leads to curves in the opposite direction. Over the entrance to a small chapel in front of the villa there is a carved stone shell. I had found another one on a stone mantelpiece in the mezzanine. I felt it was a symbol I could use to bring continuity through the house and garden. The base of the fountain would follow the curves of the shells with points facing down the four paths leading to it, giving me clear lines from the centre, to follow in the rest of the garden.

Although the journey from the Borro to Verona had been brief!, the queue at the entrance was already long. While waiting our turn I noticed people around us had tickets by invitation. We didn't, as it wasn't an open fair but just for trade. Ferruccio left me to keep our place and went to investigate. He came back looking pleased so I imagined everything was fixed. As it drew nearer our turn he said, 'Whatever anyone says just keep walking.'

He handed over our ticket and the young lady remarked, 'This is for one person.'

'This is my secretary,' Ferruccio said and marched me through the gate.

'Signorina, signorina,' she called after me; Ferruccio's hand was firmly in the centre of my back.

After a while, when it was safe, I made to turn back. Ferruccio asked, 'Where are you going?'

'I just want to thank her for the "Signorina", no mean compliment for a woman with five children.'

'*Cammina*[1]!' he said with a laugh, and we did – all morning to no avail. This was a trade fair, and more industrial than cosmetic. We stopped to rest our weary feet and had a sandwich sitting on a stool at the bar.

There were just a few more places to look. We came across a stand marked with a big sign, 'Garden Ornaments Stone', imagining it was English, I was disappointed. Here was what I wanted. But it would be like bringing coals to Newcastle, and very expensive with the shipment and so completely defeating the purpose. I took a catalogue and as we started to walk away my eyes fell on the words '*Lavorazione Artistica della Pietra di Vicenza*'.[2] The coals were already here and we had found Domenico Costa. We showed him the design and he said he could make it, and at a quarter of the price of the original estimate. We were in business. He came to the Borro and took measurements and a month later it was delivered. I was delirious with excitement, now everything would start to take shape. Vicenza stone is like cork when first quarried and consequently easy to carve. As it is exposed to the air it gradually gets harder. The colour, however, is not so good, very white and creamy. I was too impatient to wait for it to age. The solution came in boxes of black charcoal-like dust. Mixed with water, sprayed on, and then sponged off, it would eventually give the aged look I wanted. This is a long and laborious job taking quite a few days. (It was also very messy – I looked

1. walk
2. Artisan Workshop of Vicenzan Stone

like a chimney sweep.) This had to be done before starting the rest of the work, as the plants would be damaged and the gravel stained if done later.

We marked out the paths using old terracotta roof-tiles. Mr Mattessoni and his men worked relentlessly to get it finished by Easter. We planted a low box hedge to surround the four lawns that made up the major part of the garden and surrounded the fountain. Each corner had an inverted curve where stone stands held terracotta pots planted with lemon trees. Directly opposite the flight of steps leading down from the terrace we planted two full-sized cypress trees in the yew hedge, leaving a gap for a stone bench.

All that was left to do was the terrace. On the retaining wall we used cement again. While still damp it was marked into slabs, and pricked in the centre to look like the real thing. It didn't of course, but this didn't worry me as I intended covering it completely with a fast growing creeper called *Ficus Repens*. It clings very tightly to the wall with oval-shaped leaves in dark shimmering green with a beige-coloured underside. It has tiny pear-shaped fruit and being evergreen is ideal.

I needed a balustrade along the top of the wall. There are many to be had commercially but I couldn't find what I was looking for. I set out to find something to give me inspiration. Nothing, they were all too pretentious or too modern. One day I was waiting for some analysis in a clinic called Prosperious, which is a turn of the century villa, with a central stone staircase. I was sitting exactly opposite it, impatiently flipping through a magazine, when I noticed the columns. 'Wait, these might do.' The analysis was ready but I didn't move. I stayed drawing until the clinic shut its doors at 6 p.m. With a bit of trial and error it worked. These too needed to be screened, with just a glimpse here and there, to hide the fact they were in cement. I planted a very fast-growing rose called Francis Lester at the bottom of the wall together with the *ficus repens*. They intermingled and within a year nearly everything was covered. The old-fashioned roses grew profusely in clusters of very pale pink, almost white, creeping around the pillars of the balustrades and spilling onto the terrace paving. Unfortunately they have little scent. At intervals along the wall we made square pillars with a simple cornice to decorate them. On these we placed vases made again by Costa but, this time, antiquated by him. In summer they were filled with white geraniums and in winter with dark blue pansies. We inserted a pipe down the centre of these pillars which was then extended into the vase by boring a hole through the base for automatic watering on a drip system. The whole garden was watered automatically, eventually.

Mattessoni, I must tell you more about Mattessoni. As a man he is the typical gardener. Slow in movement, with a methodical walk, an almost exaggerated bend of the knee; kind and gentle with both people and animals, even dogs with 'bad names' will roll over for him. He is tall and robust with a ruddy complexion, and very, very slow to take offence. When he stamps the earth down around a newly planted tree or bush, it is done with complete authority. If planting by hand, it is almost a caress. He is ruthless when pruning, sniffs the earth and the air as if he were part of them, old friends in fact, the essence of a gardener. How lucky I was to find him. Yet again, he works with his wife and son. His wife Nila is the exact opposite, as often happens. Small and sparkling, hands that flutter expressively in all directions, she is the creative half, quick to understand, immediately enthusiastic. She conjures up amazing pieces of art. Using different objects from wood to fruit, vegetables, candles, whatever is needed to make that particular arrangement special and attractive. They have both been with me at all events, more or less important, in these years; always making the difference, the difficult and complicated seem easy. I think if I had to typecast them they would be the 'Gentle Giant' and 'Tinkerbell'.

All walls of the secondary houses or work buildings were originally painted yellow. We sent a piece of remaining plaster to a paint factory to be analysed. The colour seemed quite violent to me to begin with, but I was assured that this was what it originally looked like. I like covering walls with creeper or other plants. At Number 4, I covered the sides of the house with a rambling rose that is even more vigorous than Francis Lester. It is in a pale yellow with a darker centre and is called Mermaid. On the swimming pool and *limonaia* walls, we planted Golden Heart Ivy with a rich golden centre edged with green. It is not easy to grow and needs a lot of attention until it gets going. This particular ivy is allergic to dogs! Around the clock house, wisteria and jasmine – *rhynchospermum jasminoides* – both with heavenly scents, grow in abundance. The combination of evergreen and deciduous plants gives variation to the garden.

Large awnings were needed to protect the garden terrace from the sun. Facing south, it was relentless all day; the terrace had no protection from trees. We made them in green and white striped material, fixed to an electric motor – to pull them in and out by hand would have been impossible. We were advised to use an anemometer due to the severe winds blowing up the valleys in sharp gusts. It was a good idea until they developed a mind of their own. Rather like a science fiction movie, the awnings took it in turn to go in and out, first over the dining table and then the pool area. In and out, in and out, with an eerie moaning as their metal arms moved back and forth. Fortunately I could pull the plug. The system needed adjusting but eventually it worked.

The wall of the main house had originally had a sundial painted on it. We now tried to reproduce it. Sundials are very complicated; it takes a lot of calculations to work them out so they actually tell the time and are not just decorative. I didn't realise that there could be a difference in as small a distance as 10 kilometres in the same time zone. We decided to paint two, one on the villa side of the garden and one on the *limonaia*. It was an interesting experiment to see how they told the time in comparison to each other, and Greenwich Mean Time. We bought many books depicting old meridians. Ferruccio and I chose a motto each; this was the second time we were to do this. Mine was *Il tempo é l'essenza della vita ... fa tesoro di ogni instante.*[1] and Ferruccio's was *Chi mi guarda é non lavora molto presto va in malora.*[2]

Bonnie loved the garden – she was always beside me giving support and encouragement. She followed me step by step as I walked up and down sounding out ideas. I would stop and look down at her, share my thoughts and worries. She always captured the spirit of the moment, staying perfectly still and staring back as I rattled on, cocking her head as if in serious contemplation of the problem. At other times she would jump and sidle with infectious glee as if she imagined we had got it right. She sat on the wall beside me and scrutinized the work below. The garden is in a hollow surrounded by buildings so it is nearly always looked at from above: this is why I wanted it to be geometrically correct. It still isn't but perhaps that's part of its charm.

Bonnie was drawn to the fountain like a magnet. She

1. Time is the essence of life, treasure every instant.
2. He who watches me and doesn't work will soon be without.

would sit on the edge and watch the fish swim in and out of the Nymphaea leaves. It was tantalising to see their flickering silvery shapes skim the surface and then dart away. But she had learned her lesson the hard way years ago, when a puppy in Florence. There she leaned over raking the water with her paw in an attempt to catch a fish, but fell in instead. Our pond in Florence is small and not in view from the house. She was too little to get out; it could have finished badly but for the pots of Nymphaea. By the time I found her, God knows how many hours later, she was like a drowned rat with just her head sticking through the big flat leaves. She looked like a skinned rabbit, as I cradled and comforted her. I put a flat board with rungs of wood across it – like a ladder – in case she fell in again. By now she was a mature lady and didn't let temptation get the better of her.

I spent hours in the garden on my hands and knees patting down a roll of strange material. It looked and felt like blotting paper, but was in fact fabric. This was placed under the gravel down the paths to prevent grass growing through. In Italy it is called *tessuto non tessuto*. Bonnie thought this was great fun. I love this garden too; every year it grows more vigorous, every spring it bursts with life as it renews itself. New plants are added and become part of the whole as if the garden had been waiting for them. It has a special light in the evening as the shadows lengthen and the Borro village turns a golden pink with the sinking sun.

A strange occurrence happened that autumn. The garden was finished and was happily settling in, sending roots deep in preparation for the winter. The villa now needed clearing of all the old rubbish, just leaving me the bare remaining walls to work with. From the attic to the cellars, there was an accumulation of boxes, books, and every type of 'left behind'. Giovanni's new office was ready and he started to box up his *scartoffie*[1], not that he would like to hear me call them that! My birthday came around yet again. I'm the very typical Scorpio. Among my gifts there was a large flat package, obviously a picture. I thought of a photo or a portrait of the children, and thinking it must be special, I opened it last. I had no premonition of how special it really was. Ripping off the paper in my usual impatient way, at first I could not see what it was. It was faded and the light reflected on the glass. I looked closer, not understanding. It was a faded architectural drawing of my garden. What an original idea. I started to give Ferruccio a hug, saying thank you and how much I loved it, what a clever gift, I would treasure it.

He gently pushed me away. 'Look closer!'

I was puzzled but took the picture close to the light. It seemed genuinely old and slightly different from my garden though essentially the same. They must have found an old print. I looked closer still, the surrounding buildings were the same too, a little different here and there.

'Read the script in the corner.'

In the corner there was a note in old-fashioned script: *Pianta d'insieme delle fabbriche nuove e ridotte della villa dell borro-studio fatto in Firenze nel mese di agosto 1857.*[2] It took me a few seconds to take it in. My garden wasn't mine at all. Someone had designed it long before me – centuries ago. The idea had not been mine; someone had been there before me. I felt the hair stand up on the back of my neck. 'Who were you?' I looked at Bonnie, her black eyes stared right back into mine. This document was found, with others, in a small hidden cupboard, by Giovanni Ciprianni.

1. pile of rubbish
2. Plan of the group of newly constructed and redimensioned buildings belonging to the Borro villa project produced in Florence in the month of August 1857

9 Getting Permission

Permission to create as you wish is always hampered by other people's views of what is beautiful or correct. Objectivity seems irrelevant. Italy in many cases is a complete contradiction of itself. On the most exquisite sites the ugliest buildings are allowed, in others you can have a penal record for building an unobtrusive pool in a backwash. In other words it is always better to stand still and see which way the wind is blowing. Not so easy, however, when you have as big a complex as I did to govern. I made many mistakes and had to learn from them the hard way (Bonnie and I had a lot in common). While renewing a house in the Borro, which included the roof, plumbing, electricity and so forth, I obviously had to put in new pipes and lines. In doing so I was forced to cut through the roots of an ex-Christmas tree that had been planted about three metres from the building, and having flourished in an unusual manner, was now threatening to fall, having had its roots severed, on the new roof. 'Cut it down,' I cried without a second thought. Woe betide me!

Within 24 hours a helpful telephone call had been made and the Colonel of the Forestry Commission arrived on the scene of the crime. 'Who cut down this tree?'

I owned up immediately, no passing of the buck, it

stopped right at my feet. He was kind and explained that I had to have permission to cut down any tree. 'Permission takes time,' I explained. 'Without its roots and the wind around here, I could find myself with a large hole in a new roof. And in any case, can't I cut down anything within the area of a house that could damage it, by law?'

The answer was 'yes!'. In fact, I was within my rights, but many citizens don't know the law and he had to investigate all anonymous phone calls or letters. 'In future, let me know what you want to do, I'm sure we will have no problems.' I always did so after this, and he was right.

On another occasion, I was sandblasting the cellar. The original ceilings had been plastered again, an unusual thing to do in a damp cellar. This cellar leaked in many places and the plaster was corroded and coming apart. I sandblasted it off to reveal the beautiful tiles underneath, but this time the police arrived. I did not have permission to sandblast. I explained that I had no idea I needed permission.

'In this council you do,' was the reply.

'I see, would I need permission also to clean my house or dust?' I asked. 'Because this is part of my house, where I keep my wine and I'm cleaning it.'

The matter was dropped.

Later on, I removed the old *tini*[1] made of armoured cement from the tinaia. It was no longer legal to use them, no longer correct for holding wine. These now have to be made of steel. As they were free-standing, in other words, not built into or attached to the walls, I had them removed – not an easy job.

1. vats

The police arrived again. I was creating volume, without permission. 'Ah,' I replied, 'and if I move a piece of furniture in my home, or chop it up for fire wood, do I need permission?'

I was lucky, the question was dropped again. However, I didn't always get away with it – I have a nasty black blob on my penal record for putting a bathroom in the Borro shop. It is necessary, by law, as I was told, to have a bathroom in a shop: quite understandable. I wouldn't work in a shop without one. At the back there was a kind of cellar-pantry I made into a bathroom. This time I knew I was taking a risk. If you play and lose you have to pay, and I did, that's only fair. I deserved that one.

A few months later while I was looking from the terrace towards the Borro village, I saw a group of men with cameras. They were in suits, not country folk or tourists, except for one. Things must have been getting on top of me that day and I stomped down to meet them. 'May I help you?'

They were a committee of people taking photographs from Arezzo.

'Just checking!'

Later on the same day, I met them again. The gentleman dressed in a more casual way asked if he could look at a site I was working on that was of historical interest.

I said, 'Of course.'

'You see we can ask nicely,' he said.

'I know, I know', I replied. 'I'm just fed up with people putting spokes in my wheels every time I get on my bike. It is so demoralising. Why do I bother? I'm trying to do something everyone will benefit from. This village is not just ours, it's part of the Italian heritage and if we, my husband and I, hadn't taken on this huge commitment, it wouldn't have been here in a few years time. Why am I spending all my time and energy, let alone a huge amount of money?' A long *sproloquio*[1] but, as I mentioned, I was thoroughly fed up.

He looked at me, calmly, 'Don't lose your English phlegm. We should all thank you and we do. Remember the old Chinese saying, "If you sit long enough on the bank of the river you will eventually see the body of your enemy float by."' I hope I have no enemies but I did learn to stay calm.

1. speech

10 The Medieval Village and its Occupants

The Borro, as a village, is one project entirely unto itself and not separable into individual parts. To make the position clearer, the Borro village had to be presented as one package to the council of Loro Ciuffenna, in this case for permission to renovate. There were literally piles of paper, of maps and plans from every conceivable angle – the outside walls, windows and doors; the roofs with their different levels and shapes; the streets, their steps, arches, and dividing walls; all the plumbing system and how it would be regulated with cisterns and biological tanks; and the heating and gas systems according to safety regulations, and where they would be appropriately positioned. Then, of course, there were the interiors, from the cellars to the attics, all the different levels – what they were like at the time and what we intended doing in the future. We also had to submit plans of the drainage of rainwater and how it would be regimented to avoid flooding and corrosion. A geological expert made topographical charts, plans and maps.

As there were water veins, *falde*, under the ground, we had to indicate where the earth could slide again, or simply break away from the mass. The first house over the bridge to the village once had a substantial garden in front of it. Now all that remains is a small wall and a few feet of gravel leading to the front door. The corrosion was not always caused by landslides or water. The trees on the slopes surrounding the village grew tall, and having little earth and little light because of overcrowding, were brought down easily by strong winds. When their roots came away, so did earth, and so the cycle continued.

This mound of paper took time to compile before it was ready to send in for examination and, as luck would have it, the elections came around before anything was concluded. A new council meant new experts and new opinions, so it started again. Not quite back to square one, but nearly. Under these conditions, we were forced to ask for permission to do work as the need arose. The first occasion being for Antonio Bussu's apartment.

Antonio came from Sardegna with his family and was our resident mason. He and Tim Bell from Yorkshire worked as a team for two years. The world is a small place. I often think of Tim Bell back in England after having spent nearly two years in Tuscany. He now probably speaks Italian with a Sard accent. The agriculture and farmlands were not my side of the project. The only planting I ever did was decorative or in gardens. Here at the Borro there are 700 hectares, which increased over time as Ferruccio bought back more of the land that had been part of the estate. The original hectarage had been roughly 3500. Il Borro had once been a working, profitable farm. Today it is almost impossible to make money out of farming, but Ferruccio is an astute businessman and has always had a love of the land, passed down from his grandfather in Bonito, I imagine. For him, ploughing a field is a recreation and while we had only a small field in Fiesole, where my horse Ballyback lived, his weekends were spent ploughing, sowing and reaping. My horse would look on, wondering when he would ever have the use of his field. Ferruccio bought our first tractor at Fiesole nearly 30 years ago and we still have it today.

Getting back to the Borro, here was a massive project. First all the rivers had to be cleared and their banks recut. Woods had to be cleared; roads made passable again; bridges mended and some new ones made; wells turned operational; vineyards planted; old olive groves pruned and new ones made; and plantations of trees for wood and the usual crops of sunflower, corn and wheat. The Borro farm began to come back to life, little by little it stood up and shook off the lethargy of years of neglect. One job that urgently needed doing was to support the Borro village perched on its corroding hillock. Having chopped down those trees that could have been dangerous and cleared the slopes, the hillock had to be shored up permanently, no more temporary measures.

Experts were called in and a strong supporting wall was made where the original wall of stone could no longer do the job. This new wall also saved the road, which became impassable at certain times of the year. Now, however, Antonio and Tim took over the long and arduous job of hiding the armoured cement foundation and making it look like the original stone wall. They toiled all summer and many months into the winter. It is a back-breaking job, slow and demoralizing. Unlike making a brick wall, each stone must be chosen, an occasional piece of brick must be let in, and water-draining holes left, which were made of old terracotta roof-tiles. Although they were not operative, they were authentic. Antonio and Tim worked in the heat and the dust that summer with hats on their heads made of newspaper, and their bare chests became the colour of mahogany – even Tim's, which passed through various stages of red and pink first. The two were a picture. I only wish I had one. One tall and fair, one small and dark, working all day in the blistering heat under a large black gentleman's umbrella! Antonio's apartment was typical of what we did throughout the village in every house that was divided into apartments – not, I might add, by us. At street level, there are what we loosely call *cantine*[1] although they would never have been used to keep wine in. Years ago, they were probably used for keeping animals and farm equipment, and each had a small barred window in the front and back to give light and air. Originally they would have had no glass. In fact, many don't today. The floors were earthen and the walls of stone. No plaster or whitewash here. We nearly always managed to keep the original stairs in old *pietra serena*. Every roof and floor needed to be remade. Not one roof in the whole Borro was in good condition. As I have mentioned before, both the floors and roofs were rebuilt with the original materials, terracotta and wood, mostly chestnut. The big changes were central heating and plumbing. As far as was possible, we made the houses and apartments easy to run, full of light, cosy with character and pleasant to live in – all requisites for good tourism. Not that the village was a hotbed of tourism, anything but. Indeed, what we really desired was to have residents, people who really lived in the village, to make a community.

Elda and her family were the oldest living residents of the village, and go back many generations. I first met Elda a few days after we had signed the contract and the Borro was finally ours. I walked up to the village to look around and get a feel. There were chickens and a posse of cats, mostly belonging to Elda. I sat on the wall and ruminated. After a

1. cellars

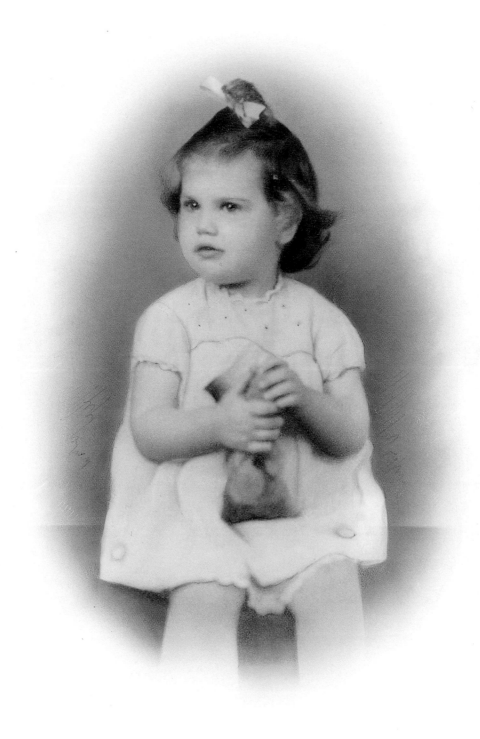

1. *The author as a child*

2. *The villa when it was purchased*

3. *Bonnie*

4. *The author carrying a wild boar over her saddle*

5. *Forest*

6. *The dining room at 'Caccia'*

7. *The swimming pool*

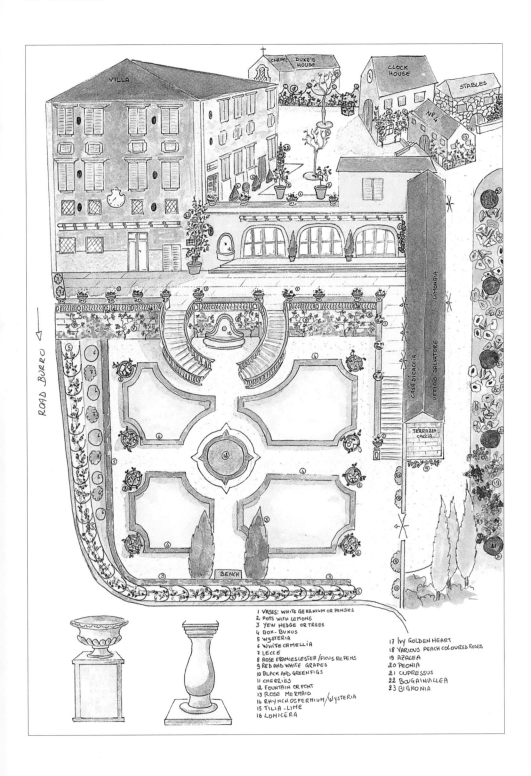

8. *Sketch of the garden*

9. *The Italian garden*

10. *The medieval village*

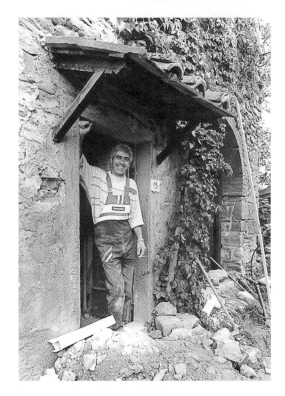

11. *Antonio*

12. *Portrait of Alessandro del Borro*

13. *The church in Borro village*

14. *Don Pasquale*

15. *Il Borro after extensive war damage*
The villa can be seen on the hill

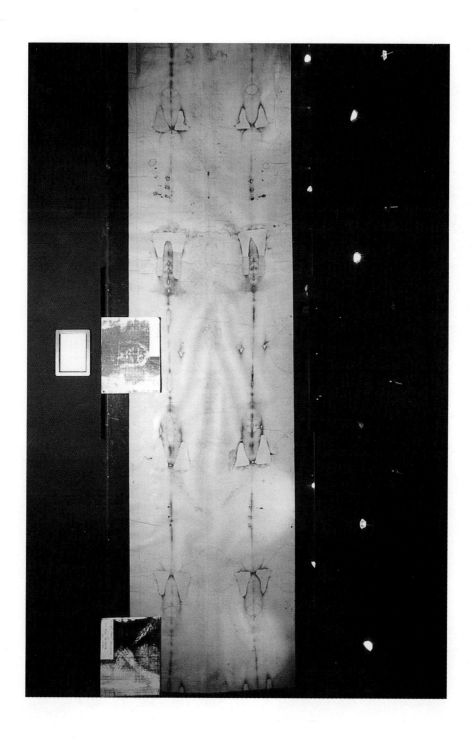

16. *Sacred shroud*

17. *Before the war*

18. *After restoration*

while someone sat beside me with bare feet. They were neatly planted together next to mine on the old paving. I looked up into Elda's face. She has a face that will always be young; not only in skin texture, but also from expression, and, most of all, radiating from the inside. Elda has an innocence born of goodness. My children loved her. 'Are you the new *Padrona*[1]?' she asked.

'I suppose you could say that,' I answered.

She looked at my feet and I looked at hers. 'Nice shoes,' she said.

'Nice feet,' I said.

We sat on the wall and she told me her life story right there and then, no introduction, no preamble, just two people who liked each other with no strings attached. She had always lived in the village, was born there and still lived in the *casa padronale* with her son and brother; this would have originally been the master house. Perhaps Alessandro del Borro himself lived in it. He lived in 1572 and the villa wasn't constructed until relatively recently, in 1840. I am not going to write about the history of the Borro. This has already been written many times – one account published recently was by Maria Christina Monti, commissioned by Ferruccio and kindly dedicated to me.

Just to put an interesting note in here (especially about the world being a small place), a few months ago I met a friend of mine in a hotel in London. I waited for her in a sitting room near the reception. There was a fire burning and I sat on a sofa in front of it. I don't know what in particular made me look back over my shoulder; on the far wall there was a portrait of Alessandro del Borro. The portrait we have photocopies of from the archives in Arezzo. There has only

1. owner

ever been one portrait of him that I know of. I asked where it was bought – at an auction.

Elda has had a hard life. At the time I met her, there was still no heating in her house, but at least she had running water. When she was young she had to carry buckets of water from the well in the valley. Going down with empty buckets was not too bad, especially in summer, but struggling up the hill against icy winds and rain in the winter must have been terrible. She was always afraid to spill any as the water she brought up the hill was used for everything: drinking, cooking and washing. If she spilled any it meant an extra journey. We reinstated that path with a handrail down one side. I was puffing away just dragging myself up, and I'm not unfit.

Elda moved into the village of San Giustino while we renovated her house. It was in dangerously bad condition. However, Elda's sister-in-law had a fatal car accident while she was there, leaving her to look after her nephew, and her two brothers. She never moved back to the village. I've always felt very sad: the Borro has lost something precious – a part of its history.

The first house over the bridge we originally used as a hunting lodge. After it was renovated, an American author moved in, Harvey Saks. He is a biographer and at that time was writing the life history of Sir George Solti, the late and famous conductor and musician. As coincidence will have it, I knew George and his wife Valerie well. Their holiday house at Roccamare in Castiglione della Pescaia, a fishing village on the coast of Tuscany, was next to ours. We spent many summers together. Valerie was from Yorkshire like I was and we had a lot in common. Our children cycled and played on the beach together. It was a very happy time full of sun, laughter, good wine and good company. There were two major difficulties however, classical and disco music. Not that George would have considered disco to be music.

As our children turned into teenagers, I decided to build a swimming pool. I wanted a little privacy; the beach had turned into a social event. Every day you would be continuously leaping to your feet, covered in sand and oil, offering your little finger or a kiss blown from fingertips. Our house was always bulging at the seams and, to cut a long story short, I needed to build a swimming pool to have an alternative to the beach.

That winter I received a telephone call from George. 'I hear you want to build a pool. No, no, Mandy, you use ours, too much noise.'

'George, I really want my own, you know, a little reprise from the beach, a lot more time to read, etcetera?'

George was far, far wiser than I, although we didn't see eye to eye on a lot of things; his always taking Valerie home early being one of them. On this occasion he was right.

That summer I had a frantic call from him. 'Horrible, horrible noise, I have never heard anything so loud in my life! We have a gentleman's agreement, I come over.' He did, and we agreed that I would not allow any noise, whatsoever, between 2 p.m. and 4 p.m. Very reasonable really, and it gave me the opportunity to blame someone else when I was dying for an afternoon rest.

I have never liked opera. I love classical music but opera, no. George tried to educate me. I sat right behind him once while he conducted *Der Rosenkavalier*. I could see him mouthing the words to Kiri Te Kanawa, and afterwards I asked him if she was inclined to forget her lines. I was, in fact, joking but my question fell on stony ground.

'You are a lost cause, Mandy.'

91

Actually, it was the fact I couldn't understand the words that I found frustrating. I couldn't let the music flow over me. I needed to participate. Indeed, a lost cause. Harvey finished his biography a few months before George died. Thinking of George today, I look back over those summers. How privileged I was to know him.

The next house, Number 12, was one of my favourites because it constituted a challenge. It was dark and unfriendly as a house. I tried to give every house a small garden. With a bit of cutting and snipping on either side, I managed to give number 12 a little handkerchief of green, with a set of chairs leading directly from French windows into the kitchen. On either side, trellis covered in creepers gave the residents the precious privacy I consider so necessary. We incorporated part of the cellar into the kitchen with a few steps descending through an archway to a pizza oven. The living room was enlarged to enclose the entrance, allowing light from two small windows to shine directly into the room from the street. With a large fire burning, brightly coloured fabrics and comfortable sofas, it was a good house.

Another author lived here, a young man called Paolo. He came from the hill town of Anghiari and wrote plays and books. Later on in the summer season, he invited us to a play in Anghiari, not written by him, although he had taken part in its production. Here you really participated, almost like a pantomime, but more so. Tables were set up around a small square in the oldest part of the town. While we ate our dinner the play was enacted around us. Suddenly a window was thrown open, the light was bright, the head and shoulders of an older woman hung out calling to a man near me. He leapt to his feet and started gesticulating and shouting back; then jumping over the bench he stumped off.

The play had begun. You never really knew until the last minute who was an actor and who was part of the audience. As the story unfolded, it was difficult to concentrate on food, although it was good. It was the most amusing and entertaining evening at the 'theatre' I have ever experienced. The comedy could not have been played without the audience. Everyone chattered to everyone else. That evening the play finished with dancing, all inhibitions having disappeared along with the second course. I heard a man at another table say, '*Io vado a ballare con lei*,' and as he advanced in my direction he offered his hand and said in broken English, 'You a like to dance with a me?' I smiled back sweetly. He must have believed I didn't speak Italian, having interpreted most of the evening for my guests who were English. Now I was going to do some acting of my own.

The next house along the street was not ours. It belongs to Marta and Gilberto. Marta is the niece of Don Pasquale, the village priest. Gilberto and Ferruccio know each other from when they were boys at school together. I met Marta the first time I walked down to the Borro. There is a restaurant before the bridge that she and Gilberto ran. She came out on to the covered veranda, used for eating outside, with a view of the old bridge and the village. Looking down at me she said hello, as simple as that. It happens in life, although rarely, I'll admit, that you meet someone you feel you have always known. She is very pretty with a halo of dark curls which naturally go their own way – she continuously runs her fingers through it, tucking rebellious strands behind her ears. She also has very dark eyes and a quick, easy smile. Marta is quite unique, always merry and laughing. She and Gilberto are a kind of aunt and uncle to all the villagers, ready at any time to fix a leak or mend a fuse. Gilberto is military-like man with a moustache and a very caustic, but amusing, sense of humour. He can make you laugh even when you don't want to. They make a great pair. Eventually they gave up the restaurant, and Marta came to work for me, running our shop Il Borro a Casa. Their house and Don Pasquale's house were the only two in the village we didn't own.

We reinstated an old *forno*[1] under Number 16. In the old days, this must have been used by all the villagers to make bread. Of course, bread ovens and pizza ovens are roughly the same – they both burn wood, which is one commodity there is no lack of in the Borro. Marta and Gilberto would bring up tables and organise evenings in the street or the little square next to the church. Gilberto worked the ovens making pizzas, which was everyone's favourite. Marta usually made a pasta dish, and everyone brought something. There was quite a community of foreigners at the Borro by now, but language seemed to be no barrier. Wine and laughter are great equalizers. Sometimes when the Stoneys were there, our resident pilot and engineer from Ireland with his wife Sandy, there would be Irish gigs and dancing, Paolo would join in with abandon and Antonio would laugh and clap his hands in tune with the music. The next morning there would be a few people nursing hangovers around the bar in the restaurant. Marta was always sympathetic, Gilberto less so as he was teetotal.

Number 16 is above Antonio's apartment with an entrance and garden at the back looking down the valley to where the well is (the path down to it leads from their garden). I joined the kitchen and living room with a central archway. The

1. oven

rooms were still essentially separate, but by joining them with an open arch instead of a doorway, it created a light and friendly atmosphere. A big, jolly fire crackling away between two sofas could be seen while working in the kitchen, and someone sitting reading by the fire or children watching TV could chat with whoever was in the kitchen. The rooms kept their own identity although they were joined. I like this solution for dark rooms and adapt it wherever possible. The kitchen should be the heart of the house. Antonio's wife, Anna, was particularly pleased when we renovated this apartment as the old floors were in such bad repair they sent a continuous shower of dust and grit down below, which was soul-destroying for someone as house-proud as Anna.

Casa Berti, as we called it, adopting the name of the last resident, was on the next corner. It had originally been a hospital. I will never understand how. It was a tiny house, straight up and down. There were no real ceilings, just floors made up of planks of wood and ladder-like stairs. As you came in from the outside, there was just the one room with two small windows and the ladder up. The next floor consisted of one room, a small bedroom and a tiny bathroom. Then up again and, through a hatch, you found yourself in an attic. You could only stand upright in the centre part of this because of the low eaves. I pondered about this house for a long time. With a solid staircase and doors, there might be more privacy but a lot less room, and you could hardly rent out a house with stairs that were the equivalent of a ladder. You would really need a hospital then. But on the other hand, it only had one small bedroom.

Standing up in the central part of the attic, having clambered through the hatch, I looked out of the two small, arched windows. It was like being up in the crow's nest. It had atmosphere and character, and that's when the idea came to me. First we made a proper staircase using the far wall opposite the entrance, straight up to the first floor, across and then up again. The stairwell itself took up part of the space under one side of the attic, so the new wall and door were not in the lowest part of the room. The door was small, and you had to stoop, but even a big man could do it with ease. On the other side of the room under the eaves I had a bed made, with fitted hanging cupboards either side. The bed was bigger than the average single bed, about 200 centimetres long by 120 centimetres wide. With a light on the inside wall and curtains to pull on the outside, you could be completely snug and private. Just like in the Navy! This method of using space under low eaves for beds has been used again and again, and always successfully, especially when used for children's rooms. I finished the attic with a chest of drawers in the highest point, a sofa against the wall and a TV. The rest of the house, in essence, remained the same. I added a stove in the corner of the living room on a *pietra serena* base. I discovered stoves were an excellent method of heating and, at the same time, gave off a merry, warm glow. The ground floor was made into one big kitchen which you walked straight into from outside. Here was a fire, again with a *pietra serena* mantle, and a round table and chairs for dining. As simple as that, and yet this house, Casa Berti, is one of the favourites to rent.

Casa Berti was unusual in many ways. Just down a few steps on the street side, and you would find yourself in the *cantine* and another world – the world of Pinocchio. As you entered the cellar it was pitch dark: just a few rays of daylight filtered their way through a small window and illuminated the stone wall here and there. The atmosphere was chilled and damp. In the winter, water drips and echoes on the stone floors. As you entered, before descending the few steps, there was a sign with an arrow indicating you should push a button. If you dared, you would find yourself surrounded by Lilliputian figures telling a story. Eight glass windows allowed the viewer to peep into the house of Geppetto as he carved away, or meet the fox and the cat sauntering down the road laughing behind their paws, or the great whale in a rough stormy sea. On emerging into the street again, daylight would blind you. Looking back at the simple dark doorway it would seem possible. I wonder if it was once a children's hospital, all those years ago. Do the walls still hold their fantasies and feverish dreams?

I'm leading you by the hand as carefully as possible through this medieval village. It is not easy to imagine through someone else's eyes. Up until now, we have been travelling along a narrow street that bends its way upwards. The street is boarded on one side by a low wall that has the valley beyond it, and the houses we have visited so far are on the other.

Casa Berti is on the corner of the first intersection. Our street, however, continues upwards a few more metres to a major crossroad. Opposite Berti there is an old church, much older than the one we use today in the square. Piazza del Duomo as Don Pasquale calls it, is small, with a peaked roof made of terracotta tiles of course and a round window that would have once been of stained glass. We combined the old church and the *cantina* of the next house to form our shop. This group of buildings are in a recess, a very strategic position isolated between two streets. Now we have reached the top of the hill. Visitors stop, puffing away, to get their breath and rest their weary legs, sitting on the wall. Right in front of them is the shop with its three glass doors. A large black sign with 'Il Borro a Casa' written in white swings in the wind. It is an almost obligatory stop for a first-timer, and once sitting on the wall you cannot possibly avoid looking at the shop, a captive audience. How fortuitous!

This building is painted strong terracotta pink. Nothing to do with me, I found it like that. I also found *rhynchospermum* climbing all around the entrance and the windows of the first floor. The main entrance to the shop was an arched doorway reached by two descending steps, a real nuisance when there was heavy rain which inevitably caused flooding.

11 Don Pasquale and the War

There is only one true protagonist in this story and that is Don Pasquale Mencatini. He has lived and breathed the Borro and its people for more than 60 years. A small man with endless energy, still a good crop of grey hair at 89, glasses hanging on a pair of enormous ears and an impish smile that reminds you of his niece Marta. His hands are small and delicate and always seem to be cold. (Cold hands, warm heart the saying goes.) He usually wears a cardigan or a jacket with a simple silver cross to indicate his calling. When he is working in overalls, covered in paint, or pieces of electric wire, and with artificial moss and sawdust sticking to his hair, you would have no idea at all! One evening, while doing some watering in a pair of old overalls, his little dog Briciola (which means crumb) at his feet, a woman passed by and asked him if he was employed here. He said he was, which was, strictly, the truth.

Briciola wore a bell so you could always find Don Pasquale. She reminds you of a Punch and Judy show: short of leg like a terrier, slightly rotund around the middle, curly black and white hair, and a curling wagging tail waving in the air like a banner over her back. She had one ear up, one down and one black eye. She was always with him as he drove at great speed to all his parish duties and

99

commitments. Don Pasquale's driving is the only fiendish thing about him. Bonnie and Briciola were the best of friends.

Don Pasquale was born at Soci near Bibbiena in Casentino, part of the mountain range that forms the backbone of Italy. He was born in 1912 and was the second of three sons. His eldest brother became a missionary in China and his younger brother joined their father Quartilio's profession and became a tailor. Don Cesare Mencatini was two years older than Pasquale and had a great influence on his life, I could almost say radically. Don Mencatini embraced his vocation at a very early age. Having been shown some pictures of missionaries at school, he knew immediately that this was his destiny. He left home at twelve for the seminary in Cortona. Two years later, Pasquale followed him. Certainly, he was influenced by his brother and yearned to be with him. Don Pasquale's brother Cesare arrived in China in 1937 and was killed there in 1941. His name is on a list of priests and missionaries to be made blessed. This list is at the Vatican and is very slowly being processed. They are currently at those who died or were martyred in 1936. 'Padre Cesare Mencattini, Missionario Martirio.' Don Pasquale always says he has a direct line to 'His ear' through his brother. I believe him. Don Pasquale's vocation was just as deeply rooted. However, his mission was here in Italy among his own people. Always creative, he started writing poetry very young. He was encouraged at the seminary and his gift bloomed. One of his first literary forays was translating the 'Favole di Fedro' from Greek into Italian.

His humour and understanding of the lives of men and women and their families is fundamental and acute. This comes through clearly in his other books and poems: *Due*

Risate al L'Aria Aperta, *La Suposta* and *Il mio Album*.[1] This last work is written in the Aretino dialect and is a collection of his poems which give true insight into the primitive and rural life of the peasant farmers, their hopes, fears, joys and sorrows. Such a love of life shines through these poems that they are unique and a tonic to read. Each year at Christmas he writes a few lines in which to convey his Christmas wishes. In 1993 it went like this (my translation):

> This year the good pheasants we eat
> Don't have blue blood in their veins.
> They too being subject to comings and goings,
> Have passed from Duke to Ferragamo.
> Even without the noble crest.
> A good pheasant is ideal
> For forgetting your troubles and
> Celebrating Christmas.

After Cortona, Don Pasquale moved on to the seminary at Arezzo. It was here he started to paint. I have never seen any of his work done when a young man but I imagine he must have been in great demand while he was studying. Here at the Borro his house is full of portraits; they are very startling and effective. The character he brings to his portraits is more than intuitive. There is a deep understanding of what is going on in the mind, and it shows. One of the portraits is quite recent. It depicts the Bishop Carraro and it reminds me of when I first met him.

   Don Pasquale asked me to come and meet the new Bishop of Arezzo on his pastoral visit to the Borro. All new bishops must go and visit their flock, even as tiny a parish as the

1. *Two Laughs in the Open Air*, *The Suppository* and *My Album*

Borro. It was a bleak winter's day, pouring with rain. The clouds were so low they seemed to be caught on the steeple of our little church. The new Bishop was a Capuchin monk from Florence. Dressed in a simple brown habit, he had a serene, kind face with a dark beard and a vague resemblance to Padre Pio.

I invited him to come and have tea. After the rain had stopped, he said he would like to walk. Darkness had fallen and we walked along, the wet road barely illuminated, splashing through puddles unseen in the gloomy dusk. We took a short cut through the cellar with its enormous vats, unfortunately no longer in use. Then another short cut through the stables.

On the wall hung an old print of St Antonio the Hermit with the wolf. Not St Francis of Assisi, although it is relatively near, and not just put there for the Bishop's visit – he is my favourite saint. Pinocchio started braying immediately, pushing his little body up against the door. Forest, however, leant right out and looked enquiringly at us. In the dim light there was a beautiful Andalusian foal, braying. Bishop Monsignor Carraro looked over the door and was delighted!

We went up into Number 4 and Beppina gave us tea. A wind had blown away the rain, but now it began to blow in earnest. Great gusts rattled the shutters, moaned down the chimney and made the fire burst like tiny fireworks. We sat on a big sofa sipping tea and dunking biscuits. The dogs sprawled at our feet lost in their dreams, with twitching muscles and puffing lips, oblivious and completely relaxed in the presence of our eminent guest. The light dimmed and then came back to life as the wind shook the wires overhead. The air was pungent with the smell of damp wool and hair. We were at peace in that little room off the kitchen. Safe from the elements, we waited for Don Pasquale to arrive with the car. The Bishop wore sandals with socks to keep him warm, which were now soaking wet. I had difficulty getting him to accept a pair of Ferruccio's old brogues, at least to get him home. Ferruccio's old brogues looked incongruous with his simple habit which billowed out as he hurried to the car. I smiled, and wondered if he had ever taken tea before, or dunked biscuits; who knows? I only met the Bishop once more, fleetingly, at a big occasion in Arezzo where he looked slightly bewildered. The Bishop's stay at Arezzo was short. He moved on to become the Bishop of Verona. Don Pasquale says, 'One day he will be a Cardinal!' It takes one to know one.

Don Pasquale first came to the Borro as parish priest in 1941. It was an unforgettable introduction year, and he never left. At first he was parish priest only to the village of the Borro, 600 souls in all. San Giustino, where there was roughly the same number of parishioners, was under the care of Archiprete Don Pietro Viviani,

In 1941, the Borro estate held 72 *podere*.[1] In the Borro village at that time, all the houses but three were then occupied by peasants. One was a tailor, one a shoemaker and the last a carpenter, the former being Marta's grand-father, who lived in the same house Marta and Gilberto live in today. Marta's mother Tina had married Ugo-Elio, Don Pasquale's younger brother.

The Borro was one big working estate, almost totally self-sufficient. The *poderi* mostly worked on the feudal system of *mezzadria*, a system where the farmers, or peasants, worked the land and gave half the crop to the landowner. This is no

1. farms

longer done. It obviously couldn't work in modern society and was unjust in certain circumstances.

It was a big enterprise. Opposite the villa, across the road to the Borro, was a large yard surrounded on three sides by buildings made of brick and open on one side with thick square columns. This yard is where the forge was located, and where farm equipment and machinery were kept, although most of the ploughing was still done by oxen. They were long-legged, white beasts with humped shoulders where the yolk was placed, a heavy piece of loose skin at their neck, large horns and, usually, a ring in their nose. They are famous throughout the world for their meat, the Chianina Toscana. They needed shoeing like horses to do their work and the forge was kept busy making these shoes and mending and sharpening equipment like scythes and hoes, making metal grilles for windows and a multitude of other objects used on a large farm.

It must have been a hive of activity with steam from the forge alternately hiding and revealing sweating men banging the anvil with white-hot iron. There would have been horses whinnying, oxen lowing, the clatter of hooves on stone, men's voices raised. The entrance to the yard was opposite to that of the cellar, and was therefore directly connected to the working area of stables, pigsties, cow byre, *tinaia*, and *granaio*. In the house we were using, Number 4, lived the gamekeeper. In the clock house there were two families of peasants, and above the *tinaia* the underfactor had his apartment. The *fattoressa*[1] managed the villa, using the top floor for her living quarters, with a large kitchen and eating area where she fed a number of employees everyday. She also had the use of the mezzanine, with three small bedrooms, one tiny bathroom, and a sitting room for farm

---

1. farmer (f)

guests, an occasional technician that needed to come for a few days for the wine or the oil, veterinary surgeons, or estate inspectors. The ground floor was used almost entirely for the accounting and administration offices. The low house opposite the villa, with the chapel, was the factor's house, where he lived with his wife. The *fattoressa* and the factor had two distinct roles, which were never held by husband and wife. In between the chapel and the factor's house, in the same building, was situated the *frantaio*, a very important facility. Here the olive presses were kept. Olive oil is, and was, a precious commodity.

Below the forge there were another two houses connected with an outside oven where a large family of peasant farmers lived called Detti. Under them, still descending the hill, was the grocer's shop and elementary school. Then up across the bridge and you were in the Borro, with the church and Don Pasquale. Everything needed was there, and all connected in easy successions. This was how Don Pasquale found the village in 1941.

The next part of the story is written as Don Pasquale recounted it to me.

3 July, 1941

A hot summer. Major Ludwic Weigan arrived at the villa with a group of soldiers. The main command, under a general we don't know the name of, was at Castiglion Fibocchi eight miles down the road in the direction of Arezzo. Part of the estate was, and still is, in this council. All the people working and living in the villa ran away except for the factor and his wife Rita.

4 July, 1941

Major Weigan came up to inspect the village accompanied by a beautiful Alsatian called S.S. (He must have had a sense of humour because the dog, although very well trained, was good-natured.) Ludwic was good looking, so much so that Don Pasquale mentioned that if he had been a woman he would certainly have looked twice. Not very tall, blond and blue eyed, elegant in his immaculate uniform.

Don Pasquale stood at his open doorway at the top of the hill and the major, on approaching him, gave a military salute, and continued on his round without a word spoken between them. At two o'clock that same day a *pattulia*[1] gathered the men of the village in the main square, just outside Don Pasquale's house. They were then incarcerated in the forge yard. Don Pasquale was not included in the round up, but he insisted on going with his men. The women and children were left behind.

Before leaving the square Major Weigan announced, 'If any man is thinking of taking flight, remember our bullets are faster.' Don Pasquale had hidden his old father in the attic, but he was eventually found and added to the group in the yard. A few hours later the Archiprete Don Piero Viviani from San Giustino and other male parishioners were added to the compound. That same day, an officer came to inform them that a lorry of German soldiers had gone into the Pratomagno in search of partisans, and for every German killed, ten of the men in front of him would be executed. As night drew on, the village women were allowed to bring straw for the men to sleep on.

5 July, 1941

The next morning Don Pasquale asked for an interview with the major, and, after some insistence, obtained it and

1. patrol of soldiers

was taken to the villa. He asked the major for an explanation as to why the villagers had been imprisoned in the forge. The major explained that they were being kept as hostages against a partisan attack. Don Pasquale managed to have about half the men released. The old and ill mostly, including himself and his father.

6 July, 1941

The following morning the major sent for Don Pasquale. He was taken to the main room on the ground floor of the villa where two men lay gravely ill. The major took a pocket dictionary out of his trousers and pointed to the words *fosforo* and *bomba*[1] and giving Don Pasquale a great push out of the door shouted after him, '*Partigiani non buono.*'[2]

Later on that same day, 37 men from San Giustino were taken to an area called L'Oreno, named after the river running through, on the road near Castiglion Fibocchi. The men were not lined up in the usual executionary fashion but just pushed into a bunch and shot. Five brothers fell together, the youngest, being trapped underneath, unharmed. He lay, with his brothers' brains spilled all over him, not moving even when kicked. In this way he saved himself. He was the only one to survive that day. Don Piero Viviani, the Archiprete of San Giustino, had originally been included in this group, but a soldier pulled him off the lorry at the last moment – perhaps he was a Christian and didn't want to kill a priest. The young man who survived is said to have never recovered from the shock of that terrible day, but he was not from the Borro and Don Pasquale cannot confirm this. The bodies were left in the sun for two days. Finally, Don Pas-

1. phosphorus bomb
2. The Partisans are no good

quale managed to ask the major for petrol and masks to burn them. The major refused, saying the Germans buried their dead, and he should do the same.

12 July, 1941

Don Pasquale and the Archiprete Piero Viviani were taken together to the German general at Castiglion Fibocchi. They were obliged to organize a civil defence warning system. Every man and boy had to wear a white armband and line the road in intervals of two to three metres. They carried any kind of metal object that, when banged together, would make a noise. They used mostly pan lids. If any partisan showed himself they were to make as much racket as possible. This continued for three days, 24 hours a day.

15 July, 1941

Just as dawn was breaking on Saturday, Don Pasquale was summoned to the villa. The major informed him that he and his soldiers were leaving – many British aeroplanes had been seen the day before, flying low overhead taking photographs. He warned it was very possible that they would drop bombs. Don Pasquale was in a quandary. The Germans were finally leaving but there was a new and immediate threat from the air.

16 July, 1941

At about 10 a.m. the next day the first bomb hit the Borro, destroying most of the *lavanderia*.[1] The *lavanderia* was the public washhouse, a low construction built of stone near the path down to the well. The villagers panicked. Don Pasquale gathered them in the square then marched them as quickly as

1. wash house

possible through the house opposite, Number 27, and out the other side through the vegetable garden and down a narrow path cut into the hillside.

The second bomb hit what used to be the 'Company' church. Now it is where Don Pasquale has his famous Nativity. The 'Company' was a group of *laici*[1], men who took part in and organized church events, such as processions and funerals, ready to be of assistance to the population in times of need.

From the bottom of the hill, Don Pasquale led his people down the Valley of the Fairies to a prefabricated refuge called L'Oreno shelter. Here they remained for the next few days.

20 July, 1941

During the night the Germans returned to the villa and mined it. They placed the mines on the side next to the road so that as it fell it blocked the road with rubble and slowed down the Allied advance. The main road from Arezzo was now useless for tanks, as all the passable bridges had been blown up. The explosion was earth-shattering, the people in the shelter deafened. Everyone was terrified; no one knew what catastrophe had overtaken them now. They sat, in awful silence, not moving, just waiting. Eventually, Don Pasquale ventured out to investigate. The Valley of the Fairies is close to the villa. There was dust everywhere. He remembered seeing huge tanks grinding their way over the rubble with no hesitation at all.

That day, 31 July, 1941, Don Pasquale led his people home. First the Germans left, then the Allies, leaving the field open for the partisans. The head, or 'Capo' for this area was one called Roule.

1. laymen

It is not difficult to imagine the mental state of the population. First condemned to a reign of tyranny under the fascists, then forced to bear the yoke under German bondage, finally the Allies, who however welcome, were still a foreign presence on Italian soil. The internal turmoil and conflict in every man, woman and child who lived through this time was great – the sorrow of loss, the physical pain caused by years of battle and hardship, the uncertainty and stress that had become part of everyday life. The muddled emotions of relief and release, common in the aftermath of war, turned to rage, becoming an uncontrollable volcano that burned for justice and revenge. The obvious target was the Borro's factor. He was a fascist cardholder, a subscribed member of the party that had caused such horror. He had not been taken with the other members of San Giustino to die. He had remained at home when the Germans arrived. Now he was to pay for it, unfortunately with his life.

Cianchi, the factor, lived in the long low house extending backwards from the chapel, a pretty house with a hidden garden. His wife Rita was expecting a baby. It should have been a happy time, peace had come to extend her hand to all, but Cianchi knew he was in danger, no amount of hand shaking was going to dispel the black cloud that hung over him. He took the precaution of having a peephole installed in the door and insisted the gamekeeper lived with them.

Roule and his men didn't go directly to the factor's house. First they collected the *sottofattore*, who was living above the *tinaia*. It must have been dark, or their movements would have been noticed. Creeping round the side of the house, Roule made Giunti, the *sottofattore*, ring the bell, keeping well out of sight himself. The gamekeeper looked through the peephole and saw only the *sottofattore*, and gently opened the door. Roule went in, gun drawn, to find Cianchi ill. Cianchi was rudely pulled from his bed and dragged outside with the *Guardia*. Roule then went back in to steal all he could find, from shoes to house linen, the most significant being the *trousseaux*, made by Rita, for her new baby. Cianchi was taken under the Borro bridge and along a track bringing them out on the seven bridges road, exactly where the 36 men from San Giustino had died. Cianchi died with five bullets in him.

Gradually life at the Borro returned to normal. If you can call it normal, as the world was still at war.

Don Pasquale looked at his domain. The *Chiesa della Compagnia* was badly damaged and most of the *lavanderia* was gone. It was time to begin again, to work together with a will to create a new and better future, to learn from mistakes and to go forward together with tolerance and patience. What better time to start than Christmas? For Christmas is the birth of new and eternal hope. Don Pasquale created a Nativity to bring this moment into the everyday lives of his people. It depicted the people that worked the land, cared for the animals, fired the forge, made the wine and olive oil, the carpenters who built the Borro and the housewives who washed, carried water and cared for the children. It was all there in miniature, all moving like magic, the people going about their daily chores. Milk squirted from cows, flames leapt from the fire, water gushed down the hillside.

At the same time, the religious and historical side of the Nativity was emphasized, taking the viewer back to Galilee, a storm on the lake, a deluge of rain, sudden darkness with the voice of the angel crying out, then lightning flashing: it was dramatic and spellbinding. At Christmas, and right up to Epiphany on the sixth of January, the queue of people to see Don Pasquale's Nativity reached right down the hill.

12 The Borro Village Completed

The Borro is famous for another religious feature, the Sacred Shroud. The *Sacro Sindone* was presented to the last king of Italy, who in turn gave it to the church. It is now kept in Turin and can only be viewed once every 25 years. It is an amazing relic and demands great reverence. When you find yourself standing in front of it, the effect is spine-chilling, I imagine, whatever your beliefs are. His Royal Highness Amadeo d'Aosta is the only member of the Italian Royal family remaining in Italy; he obtained one of the only two life-sized perfect photocopies of the *Sindone*. This he donated to Don Pasquale and the church at the Borro. To begin with it was placed behind the altar where it could hardly be seen. The Borro church was rarely locked so security was non existent, and eventually it would need to be removed while the church itself was renovated.

There are some steep steps running down the side of the church to the back of the building. Here, hidden from view, was the village dump. Everything from gas cylinders to refrigerators could be found there, as well as the usual building debris such as old basins, tubes and leftover cement. Hidden in the far corner of the yard was a small door. Don Pasquale opened it and led me to a small room which had for years been used for storage. It needed work done on it, but was perfect for the *Sacro Sindone*.

We turned the dump into a garden. Roses climb up the back of the church, wide steps lead down to a small patio with benches and decorative trees for shade. It is a secluded, peaceful place in which to meditate and contemplate the uninterrupted view down the valley. We planted rosemary, lavender, and jasmine and all those herbs and plants that bloom in the early spring, filling the light breeze with their scent. So people come, from far and wide, to the Borro once more.

Many of the people that come to the Borro are city folk, and Don Pasquale decided to educate them in country traditions and customs. His house, as I mentioned earlier, is at the crossroads, or fork, at the top of the hill. A large house, perhaps on a par with Elda's, which would be correct considering it belongs to the church. The wall facing down the valley is almost like battlements. As the Borro was once a castle with a drawbridge to protect it, this rings true as well. On the ground floor of his house, Don Pasquale created the *mestiere*, which means trades. Each scene represents an important part of country life and its industries. The miller grinding the flour and storing it in sacks; the grapes being crushed and the juice pouring into vats to ferment and make wine; the pressing of olives to make oil; pigsties with litters of piglets; and the oxen being shod for work in the fields. There were also the instruments and tools used for these crafts, the plough, the hoe and the scythe. These could be touched and marvelled at. The city folk, especially their children, experienced another dimension of life in that small room belonging to a country priest.

Let me continue with our tour of the village. By now you

nearly know it all. There is one long block of houses that goes from Number 27 in the square and finishes with Elda's house on the far side. But let's walk around the square first. Number 27 faces the square and Don Pasquale's house and you enter it by going down a couple of stairs into the living room. There is a large kitchen at the back on the ground floor. Upstairs there is another largish room with a fireplace and a large pair of French windows looking over the small square below. There are two bedrooms behind this one with an ensuite bathroom – which is unusual as it bridges two houses, Number 27 and Number 23 behind. These bridge-rooms were made in the old days to steady the houses on either side. Something to think about while lying in the bath!

We had a couple living here for two years. She was from Finland and a pianist; he was from South Africa and an opera singer. They travelled a lot giving concerts, but when they were at the Borro they used the room overlooking the square as their music room. Ingrid played their grand piano – it was, in fact, their baby – and Robert sang. His voice soared over the rooftops and cascaded down again like blossom petals. People would stop in the square to listen. If there was a busload of tourists, they would stand enraptured, clapping heartily when the aria was over. Robert would come to the balcony and bow. Ingrid also gave piano lessons. Then endless scales would ricochet off the walls and we would listen to the same few notes repeated time and time again.

One Christmas, Ingrid and Robert decided to form a Borro choir. We were a ragged bunch: Antonio and Anna, Marta and Gilberto, William and Sandy Stoney, and I. We erratically practised singing Christmas carols. We were to give a soirée. The church was full that Saturday before Christmas – even people who had not been invited came. It

114

was bitterly cold and our breath came out in white puffs. It was really quite embarrassing how bad we really were, partly from stage fright, partly from cold, and mostly from lack of talent. We struggled on with Robert conducting and Ingrid playing the piano. I distinctly remember examining the roof, noting where it leaked, then the cracked and missing window-panes, the chipped and broken *pietra serena*. Worst of all, someone had replaced the original choir stalls behind the altar with painted *faux bois* instead; but when all was taken into consideration, the greatest challenge would be to heat it. Robert was a large, robust man and barrel-chested, with a head of blond hair and high colour to his cheeks. When he threw back his head, opened his arms and sang, he was very impressive. Ingrid was gentle, soft-spoken and rather bohemian in her way, with long dark hair in a plait down her back. We became friends, and I was sad to see them leave. The cold in the winter finally beat them. Robert was one of those people who complained that the gas to heat the house cost more than the rent. It was true. The question was, which was too expensive?

After the Christmas carols, we all went over to the club for a celebratory drink that was sorely needed, and deserved, by both singers and audience. The club was a large room over the shop with two windows covered in jasmine. Having done the usual restoration, I furnished it with a sofa bed, TV set, a large bookshelf, carpets and six card tables and chairs. There was also a small bedroom and bathroom at the back. We used this mostly for art exhibitions, but otherwise the *Borrigiani* used it for occasions like this one, or when they had extra people to stay. It has been very successful.

There are two other houses in the square, one being above the club with a separate entrance directly off the square. This is where the Principessa Giulia Pignatelli lives with her two dachshunds, Pizza and Potolino. Giulia does not spend a lot of time at the Borro, at least not while I was there, but when she was at home, her presence was certainly felt. Flowers and plants appeared everywhere. On the steps, in the square and in window boxes. She was always tanned and pretty, smiling and jolly. Gilberto would help her with luggage and settling in, while she would sit on the wall chatting to Marta. Her great friend was Luciana, who originally had the house opposite her, next to Don Pasquale. Luciana came from Naples and her brother, a doctor, had the house behind Number 27, Number 20. I never did anything to Giulia's house, she had restored it very nicely herself, but Luciana's house was a mess and needed a large restoration job, taking months, so she moved into Number 26 which had just been finished. Numbers 26 and 27 would originally have been the same house. Number 26 was a pretty house over three floors. It had character but was dark, being the first house in the alley that ran across the Borro. Luciana's old house in the square was an interesting house to renovate. We developed what would have been the cellar on the ground floor into an entrance and kitchen. When you came in the front door you could see right through to the alley at the back. Like Robert and Ingrid's house, it had the main living room on the first floor, looking into the square.

There are two more houses in the alley. Number 25 is divided into two apartments, both with unusually high ceilings. This gave me the opportunity to make *soppalchi*[1], which I like. With a stair at the side it gives a private area in a room and, of course, the extra space for a bed is always useful. This type of balcony makes me think of Henry Higgins' library in *My Fair Lady*. Its nice to have bookshelves, a

1. hanging lofts

desk and perhaps a TV set or computer for anyone in a large family who wants to work or read in relative peace in this area. I've always found it a good and attractive solution to a shortage of space.

The last house in the alley was the one next to Elda's, again over three floors. It had magnificent views down the valley at the back of the Borro. The alley itself was pretty and quaint. We put some wooden benches against the walls so neighbours could sit outside their kitchens and chat to each other, just as it has been done in Italy for centuries. We planted rhynchospermum, for its dark evergreen leaves and sweet scented flower in the spring. There was a little gap between Luciana's house and Don Pasquale's on the alley side, and this I decided to turn into a courtyard. It was paved with *pietra serena* and a wrought-iron gate was placed at the entrance. I put in a wall-well with chain and bucket, not functioning of course, and filled the whole area with hydrangeas. The effect was very pleasing.

You must be getting tired, but we only have the back street of the village left. At each end there is a small house, Numbers 20 and 21, with the *orto del prete*[1] in the middle. The first house, Number 21, directly behind Elda's, has a corner plot and a large garden. The Stoneys live here, William, Sandy and their daughter Sophia. Again, it is an un-usual house built on different levels. There are several steps down to the main door, but there is another door at street level opening on to the first floor. On the ground floor there is a large kitchen and dining area that opens out to the garden, completely secluded at the back. On the first floor there is the living room and study, and two bedrooms and

---

1. priest's vegetable garden

117

bathroom on the top floor. Pretty regulation stuff; most of the houses in the Borro follow this pattern. The last house, the other end of the *orto*, is Number 20. It is very similar in floor plan to Number 21, but here there was no garden, only a footpath about 12 inches wide which had begun to crack and slide in places. With another bad winter, it would have joined the rest of the mud and rocks at the bottom of the hill, and probably part of the house would have gone with it. It was one of our first priorities to save this house. We made a structure to support a small terrace at the back of the house, with pylons of armoured cement bored deep into the ground and cases of stones and rock, which in turn, supported the house. We managed to save a couple of trees and bring them through the paving. With low walls of stone, to border the terrace, and to sit on, it gave some breathing space around the house, decorated with pots of herbs and plants. The kitchen and little sitting room lead directly onto this area. I have had dinner on this terrace many times, invited by Bepe Guerriero, the doctor, Luciana's brother. It is beautiful, especially in the evening with a light breeze coming up the valley and the smell of roses from the Sindone Garden on the left and the earthy smell of watered tomatoes and basil on the right. The valley falls away in front of it with the *balze* of yellow clay tinged pink by the setting sun. There is a dream-like quality about the whole scene, as the dust of the day begins to settle, while the glow-worms flit, here and there, in the twilight like tiny fairies carrying lanterns. It is enchanting.

We have come to the end of our tour. There are no more buildings to renovate, except the church, which I will deal with later. We made four little shops along the back street with hanging signs reminiscent of the Borro a Casa sign. These were occupied by an antique dealer, a jeweller, a saddler and a potter. The craftsmen open mostly only on weekends or by appointment. The Borro was truly returning to its origins, picking up the mantle of self-sufficiency and independence once more.

13 The Killer Instinct

One of the most irritating things, and one that spoilt the look of the village as a whole, were the electric wires marching on poles up the side of the Borro to join a gathering of TV aerials at the top. They did not fit the image, and had to go. Most of the original paving in the village was gone, in some places replaced by cement and in others it simply had never been there at all. To find old paving was difficult in small quantities and here we had a large area to cover. Ferruccio came up with the clever idea of using the old floor in the *tabaccaia*, a huge building on the upper plateau near the airfield. It had been built for drying tobacco. There are many *tabaccaia* in the Valdarno district, being prominent in the tobacco industry for generations. It is fascinating to follow the drying process, in small but tall rooms, with fires built into their floor and the rafters filled with hanging leaves of tobacco, large and flat and gradually turning brown. This had once been a prosperous industry employing many men and women. We used the *tabaccaia* to store grain and keep all the farm machinery and tractors. I put in new changing rooms and bathrooms for our workers and a new kitchen and canteen, but the floor was too good for tractor oil and cooking fat. Ferruccio had all the stone floor taken up and we used it as paving stones. It was a perfect solution. While the streets were up, large tubing was inserted for TV cables, and electric wires, leaving surplus piping in case it was needed in the future.

I planted 3000 blue irises; this traditionally Tuscan flower usually grows wild in the hedgerows and banks along the side of the roads. A mass of blue under mimosa and robina trees was striking and replaced the chickens along the brow of the Borro. Sometimes I wonder if I didn't make a mistake, perhaps chickens would have been better, but they would have never survived.

All was not sunlight and roses at the Borro. There was a mean pack of hounds that slunk away secretly to terrorize and kill the village cats. They would approach the village with absolute stealth, the mother in the advance position with her son and daughter behind in perfect formation. Their shoulders hunched and necks slung low, they were a gang of outlaws with perfect synchronization and maximum concentration, their tawny eyes glowing ever-alert to any feline movement. Every step was measured in their hunt for a victim. The Cat Killers. Most distressing, they were total lap dogs at home. Bliza, Brugo and Biga, my three eldest children's dogs. There was very little I could do about it. Here were the classic symptoms of Dr Jekyll and Mr Hyde. One day, the two younger dogs actually found a way onto the roof of the stables and killed Mandy the cat. Don Pasquale begged me to save his cat's life. Eventually the awful three-some was broken up, but not before the cat population at the Borro had been almost exterminated. Don Pasquale's cat did, in fact, survive. Bonnie, on the other hand, I am proud to say, never had the opportunity to develop this animosity. When she was a six-month-old puppy, we found a litter of kittens. She came with me daily and while I fed them, she licked them clean. The maternal instinct won over that of the killer.

14 The Countryside and its Farms

There are many farmhouses on the estate, another name more frequently used in Italy is *podere*. We had fifteen in total and I had most of them swirling around in my mind. The farmhouses could be pretty inaccessible, not if you had a jeep of course, but I've never been good at driving up steep, muddy slopes. I'd rather do it on a horse. It wasn't possible to get away often, but whenever I could Bonnie and I would be off. To begin with, she was too small to do a long ride. She would keep up very gamely, scurrying along behind Woody, but at a certain point she just stopped and sat down, pink tongue lolling out. She would then pretend to be deaf, so I would have to go back. Stretching up on Woody's front leg she would pant and smile up at me, and leaning down I pulled her up by the scruff of the neck. It became such a habit, such a natural thing to do in the end, that neither she nor Woody thought twice about it. To begin with, however, it was not so easy. Bonnie would wiggle across the pommel wanting to be carried in my arms. Woody would drop her shoulder, in typical polo fashion, and send Bonnie tumbling down. The exercise would start all over again. One day, Woody abandoned us both. We were on our way to a new house. In the spring, the little river we had to cross was much fuller and faster than usual. I was thinking, miles away.

Bonnie was, by now, fully grown and had passed this way many times before. As I went up the far bank I turned back to look for her. There she was on a rock in the middle of the stream, with water rushing past her. It must have been like the white water rapids for her. I called, 'Come on Bonnie, you can make it.' She leapt bravely into the water, but she couldn't make it against the current. Battling with all her strength, her head just above the water and her front paws beating frantically, she was swept down the river. I was off in a flash and in the water after her. Thank God it was shallow and she didn't go far before I grabbed her, soaking wet and miserable. She looked at me full of reproach as we clambered back up the bank. By now I was soaked too, looking forward to getting home and into a hot bath, but it wasn't to be. Woody had decided she had had enough and had made for home. That left Bonnie and I, two bedraggled figures, my boots full of water, to squelch our way home on foot. This was just one incident; as a rule all went well. I've spent many happy and productive hours, with my pocket notebook and pencil, getting the feel of a building in almost perfect silence. Just the comforting sound of Woody chomping the grass, meaning she was still there, and Bonnie scurrying after mice.

A house can almost talk to you: standing in ruins it will tell you through empty windows and stairs going nowhere how it was, who lived in it. Blackened holes in the walls show where fireplaces used to be, an old stone basin with water-marks indicates where a family washed and the remains of stencilled patterns on pieces of plastered wall hint at how the rooms were decorated. Watching the sun move overhead or the shadows of an old tree fall, you can almost feel a house rebuild itself, showing where the kitchen should be, so you can use a special space as a patio to catch the early sun. You can imagine a family drinking coffee and reading newspapers over breakfast. You can see where the shade will be at midday, how to get light into a dark room in winter and how to make it cosy with a fire, and which side of the house will be less noisy for bedrooms. It goes on forever, like dominoes in my mind until it all falls together.

Riding in the Borro is always inspiring. The countryside is powerful and dramatic; this is Leonardo da Vinci land. A short way down the seven bridges road there is an old Roman bridge, too narrow for two-way traffic, which must have saved it during the war. On one side before you cross, there is a really bad copy of the *Mona Lisa* with Save the Bridge! painted underneath. In the background of the famous picture is our bridge, or something very like it, with the *balze* that are typical of this region. *Balze* are where the steep sides of valleys have eroded away, leaving blazes of yellow clay. Where there is less vegetation you can find strange configurations of this yellow clay sculpted into fanciful shapes, left standing on their own like an exhibition of modern art abandoned in another era. One of my favourites is a finger pushing through the hard cracked earth pointing heavenwards, but then, of course, one thinks of Michelangelo, not Leonardo. In complete contrast, the woodland's lush foliage casts green shadows, brooks and streams tumble and bubble over grey rocks and wild strawberries grow on the bank at the side of the path.

In the spring I sit and eat strawberries till my tongue turns red. I wait for them over the weeks, watching them turn from white, to light green tinged with pink and then, finally, juicy red. They never taste as good as when you pick them and eat them sitting in the sun. Also, there are no grey squirrels in Italy, just as there are no native red ones in

124

England. Here their tails are bushy, almost black, and their bodies a glossy, glowing chestnut colour. Their ears point upwards with wisps of dark fur. Curious and fast, they bound from branch to branch overhead.

Once while I was riding Woody, we met a wild boar. Woody had been blowing and shaking her head for a few minutes, and as we turned a bend in the track, there she was with a group of tiny striped babies clustered around her. We all stopped dead still, including Bonnie, thank goodness, then with a grunt and a twist of her tail, the boar and her family were gone, hidden by the undergrowth.

There are many ways to see the countryside and the lie of the land. One of them is by air. We had an airfield at the Borro, with a long runway, just a few metres off a kilometre. William Stoney, our resident pilot, kept his aircraft, a glider with an engine, in a balloon-type hangar. I never actually went with him, but he was always generous and offered trips to anyone who was interested. His aerial photographs have been a great help to me. I have heard it is wonderful up there in a glider once the engine is turned off and the plane picks up the currents running off the Pratomagno.

I did, however, go up in a balloon. I was really put in such a position that I couldn't refuse. The experts arrived with their balloon and laid it all out in a field below the Borro. It looked incredibly big lying there on the grass, full of patches, and the basket, by comparison, looked incredibly small. I kept thinking, 'How am I going to get out of this?' If you haven't realized by now, I will admit that I am strongly adverse to heights. Although I have trained myself, over time, to go up ladders onto roofs in construction, I thought this was pushing my nervous system too far. God, I prayed, please send us a sudden storm, hail or something the balloon can't go up in. He didn't listen and after a certain amount of preparation the balloon began to fill. Gradually and silently like a massive bubble it formed and filled until it floated above the basket and its hissing jet of flame. I had heard a terrifying story about a lady who lived in Number 11, before our time, who had been very badly burned in one of these, right here at the Borro. But there was no hail, no storm, no way out. I threw my leg over the side of the basket, and Stefano, the owner of the balloon, followed. He is a jolly man, very chatty (which was a good thing, as my white-knuckled silence was less noticeable) and with a bushy black moustache. Up we went, the silence being shattered every now and then by a blast from the gas cylinder and another brief spurt of flame. The basket seemed very fragile as we continued to rise. The views *were* beautiful, the landscape *did* have another perspective from up here. The silent drifting was dream-like. I tried to concentrate on the distance rather than what was below me. I felt very vulnerable. We lifted up over a ridge thick with trees, when, nearly over, the basket caught in the top branches of an oak. I was rigid with fear but for Stefano, it was normal. A bit more gas, a snapping of branches and we were away again, making our way towards the Pratomagno. I lost my nerve. Turning to Stefano I said, 'Great! But I'd like to land now. Right now, before we get anywhere near those mountains.' We landed in a field, the basket fell on its side and I scrambled out. Oh, what joy to feel my feet on *terra ferma*. I think if I had been on my own, I would have kissed the ground like the Pope. We now have a lot of ballooning at the Borro. In the summer, rallies are organized, and watching 60 to 80 balloons take off and float away in spheres of brilliant colours against the pale sky is awesome.

Out of all the houses in the agri-tourism of the Borro, only two have been completely finished and are now operational.

Both are located at the far end of the airfield, surrounded by countryside, large gardens and swimming pools. The first is Poggio Piano with spectacular views down the valley. There is a small pond where the boar and her family had undoubtedly been drinking when we met them, just down the track. In this valley, just below the house, I planted two thousand lavender bushes, surrounding them with beehives in the hope the bees would make me lavender honey. It didn't work, they made delicious honey, but it was more millefiore than lavender. The lavender, however, was useful for drying and putting into pretty sachets for sale in the shop.

The house itself had been used as a retreat for a football team. The upper floor had not been touched, the ground floor was just one large room with a kitchen and multiple showers. It was an ugly house with little character or charm. I tried to give it some by putting a small insert into the roof with an arched window. This let light into the loft and followed a pattern I was creating. On the first floor, two flights of external steps met at a small landing. I enlarged the landing and the steps, and in place of a door, I opened a large arch to make an entrance to the apartments on either side. Finally, at ground level between these steps, I made the third arch with two small windows in the centre, giving light to bathrooms inside and character to the house. The effect was pleasing.

The best part, and my favourite part of this complex, is the old *capanna*. Originally it would have housed cows and hay. Now all that was left standing were the old weather-beaten stone walls of the central part of the building, and two arches, one above the other, at the apex of the roof. In the silence of the early hours, before the cock begins to crow, forms emerge from the dewy mist. Deer! This is one of their favourite places, a small field surrounded by woods, carpeted with lush grass. Right in front of you, groups of deer will feed. The young with their spotted coats and little wagging tails. The adults moving in their jerky, nervous way, ever ready to take flight. It is a private spectacle, precious and unique, seen only from the window of the main bedroom. On the opposite wall a small square window looks towards the airfield in the distance. A large pine tree, with branches spreading over the roof like a protective umbrella, almost blocks the view of the road leading to the house, but you can still spy a car coming five minutes before the bell will ring. My only regret is that the *capanna* is not more secluded. It doesn't have a swimming pool and garages of its own, but is a large complex. This group of four apartments and one cottage can sleep 21 people. Each apartment has its own garden with table and chairs for eating out, which is good business.

The second farmhouse to be finished and operative, Casa al Piano, was exactly opposite, across a small ravine, but, unfortunately, it was on the road. Here, again, was roughly the same thing, four apartments with a large garden area and a swimming pool. The swimming pool is interesting. The lie of the land was such that it gave me the opportunity to create a lower terrace behind converted stables, now used for barbeques, outside dining and showers. The swimming pool area is down two flights of steps, branching from a patio. It is all paved in stone with a low wall surrounding it. This gives the pool complete privacy from the house, and, in return, avoids noise for those at home.

All this area surrounding the airfield was designated to become part of the golf course but, until that happened, the field between the airfield and Casa al Piano became a racetrack for dune buggies, marked out with bails of hay. With balloons going up, airplanes coming down, and dune buggies tearing around throwing up mud, this was no docile country scene. I'll take the deer any day, but then, '*Il mondo e bello perche e vario!*'[1]

Out of the fifteen *potere* I mentioned earlier, these are the only two I completely finished like the houses and apartments in the Borro, meaning they are ready to walk into, completely furnished and fitted out with every type of convenience and necessity – right down to a Moka coffee machine. I worked on designs for other houses while doing the golf course project, but only one '*Chiocci di Basso*' along the seven bridges road had permission to start renovation.

L'Oreno uno was another house I worked on. However, I really disliked its position. It would have been a fantastic location right in the heart of a cluster of *balze*, close to the Oreno river, but slap in front of it there was the viaduct carrying the Trans-European Express. You can actually see this *casa colonica* very clearly from the train, and vice versa, and of course the noise was terrific. I worked on the designs with the architect for some time, actually going to see the new mayor of Laterina, a pretty woman with auburn hair, to discuss two things: one was replacing the *colombaia*, a small, square, turret-like room in the middle of the roof where pigeons were originally kept (most *case coloniche* had these), the other, the possibility of getting sound brakes, big green panels, mounted on this part of the train track. Unfortunately, we didn't succeed with either.

At this point we had in the region of forty beds to offer tourists. Marketing and advertising now became a major necessity, and, consequently, so did the events we organized at the Borro.

1. The beauty of the world lies in its variety

15 The Beginning of Events

One of the very first events we had at the Borro was a cross-country ride with a gymkhana in the afternoon. Salvatore, one of my twin sons, organized the sports, and I orchestrated the food with other Borro ladies, in a marquee. We never expected so many contestants – horseboxes arrived from all over the district. It was raining but they still kept coming. There were sixty equine competitors of every size and shape, plus their riders and friends. Each rider had a number strapped to their back. The route was not easy, and was made worse by the rain. Down steep, stony tracks, over narrow bridges, through rivers, along twisting paths through orchards and lastly across a muddy field. It was not a question of who did it in the least time, but who did it nearest to the time previously established. The last muddy field floored everyone. As the rain continued, the muddier it got. One robust squire, on his robust hunter, sank in up to the horse's knees. There was no question of wearing hard hats or body-protectors. Every type of amusing garb imaginable was worn. Cowboy hats, satin jockey's bonnets, baseball hats with the name of a sponsor printed on it. One man riding a beautiful Andalusian stallion had long flowing hair, a tight, short black bolero and black leather chaps studded with silver. At the end of the morning, however, they all looked the same. Muddy!

Lunch in the marquee was a hilarious occasion. There were long wooden tables and everything was steaming, both the food and the riders. I had large York hams sent over from London. When boiled, their fat was cut into diamond shapes, studded with cloves and crusted with Demerara sugar. They were then roasted in cider. Cider and Chianti make for a jolly afternoon. Every type of silly game was organized for the afternoon gymkhana, mostly in teams of two. Eating apples hanging from strings, changing jackets midway, or even horses. It was chaotic. I never expected any of the serious-minded riders to join in, but everyone did, with relish. The crowd grew ever larger as the rain stopped and the villagers from San Giustino came to join the fray.

We were lucky, *very lucky*, everything was haphazard in those early days, but no man or beast got hurt. At one point Vicky asked me to bring up Brandy Snap. I half-thought I might have a go, it looked such fun. On the way down the line of tethered horses, we passed the Andalusian who let out his macho stallion squeal, stamping his feet. The equivalent of a wolf whistle, I imagine. That was the first time Brandy and I landed in a ditch. Luckily on all four feet, and I didn't come off, but it changed my mind about competing. I wasn't going to risk life and limb on this flighty filly! If only I had remembered this, I wouldn't have my wonky wrist today. I can't remember who won the gymkhana or the combination, but I do remember who won the morning's cross country, my naughty niece Flora, on Woody.

I mentioned earlier that the Mayor of Terranuova Bracciolini, Carlo Pasquini, had asked me to take a stand at their fair, which we did. It was here that I got the idea for an antique fair at the Borro. We sent out notification to all the stand holders we could find and organized a meeting. We had to limit the number to ten stands to begin with. We had jewellery, prints, clothes, china, brass, linens and furniture. We made each individual stand with green and white awnings. I wanted to keep it all in theme. The awnings in my house were the same and also, eventually, those at the restaurant. Every month with a fifth Sunday was ours. The Borro was packed, which automatically drew other merchants such as candy and floss sellers. A solitary actor always turned up dressed a bit like Charlie Chaplin. Once money was put in his hat, he moved like an automated doll. It was all good trade. We made big posters depicting a drape in green and white strip with the oval Borro trademark. We advertised in local newspapers and finally someone from the local TV station came to get an interview. I hoped Ferruccio would do this, as he has experience, but it fell to me. I was so nervous, once I started talking to the camera, my Italian deserted me. I began to mentally question every word I said. We stopped and started umpteen times, thank God it wasn't live. Eventually, over the years, I got the knack.

Ferruccio and I were asked to be the patrons for the yearly cycle race. Now this is serious business in our area. We had meetings with the organizers, press and local TV that went on for weeks before the actual race. I have never been an avid bicycle rider, although perhaps as a child. I don't think women are, as a rule.

The start of the race was in front of our main gates. All traffic had been stopped along the course to Terranuova Bracciolini, the finishing post, about 15 kilometres away. I brought down the checkered flag and they were off. With a humming of wheels, they flashed by in their rear-pointed helmets, like so many colourful bees. That afternoon we presented silver cups on a stand in the main square at

Terranuova Bracciolini. The whole town was there. In a little shop in San Giustino, I had noticed an old photo of a cyclist holding a large silver cup. Normally I wouldn't have noticed it but, considering the circumstances, I did and asked who it was. It was Moser, one of the most famous Italian cyclists of all time, and believe it or not, he first competed on a team from San Giustino. Once I had complimented and congratulated, I was stumped for what to say, then I remembered Moser. What a coup: for once I said the right thing.

From cycling we went to vintage motorcars. One stage of a rally was held at the Borro, with a luncheon and speeches before they move onto the next. The cars were magnificent. The focal point of the day was the drive through the cellar. Ancient cars rumbling past ancient and enormous vats reaching almost to the vaulted ceiling. Men in goggles, ladies with long scarves emerged from the dark cellar in their magnificent machines, to the cheers of the crowd.

People now expected there to be something going on at the Borro every weekend. It was not unusual for people to stop and ask me in the supermarket or in the streets. We needed a car park. So we made one large enough to contain 300 cars. On special days not even this was enough, far from it.

16 The Villa

For two years the villa looked over my shoulder. Whatever I was doing it sought my attention from its dominant position. As if it could stretch out a stony finger and tap me on the shoulder, or whisper directly in my ear, reminding me at odd times that it was waiting to take its new role as our family home. From photographs it would seem a large house, but when broken down into its component parts it was not enormous and could be made very manageable. Just a *pied-a-terre* as Ferruccio would tease.

For two years I wandered around its shell, whenever I had a spare moment, taking my notebook and thinking as logically as possible about what were our needs as a family. Of course, there is a great difference between what is actually needed and what would be nice. The knack is to combine the two. I made lists of the essentials, then lists of what we would all like to do, and lastly, lists of what we might need in the future. Where we would be in 10 years time? How many would we be? Would I be a grandmother? I hoped so, many times over.

I left the lower floors for the time being – it had already been decided that there would be the swimming pool and gym – and concentrated on the two floors above and the mezzanine. First of all I had to connect them, and a narrow flight of steps down the side of the house wasn't going to be adequate. Remember, I had the old photo from before the war to guide me as to where the windows were, and their size, which consequently indicated the height of the rooms.

I started with the obvious place, the front door. It would also be the most natural place for a staircase. 'Hello, how are you? Do come in, we can leave your suitcases here and take them up afterwards. You must be dying for a drink, come through to the drawing room.' Right ... how? I had Giovanni's long corridor going from one end of the house to the other; joining the back and front. I decided to make everything revolve around itself, using this corridor to connect it all. I had my list of necessities: kitchen; pantry; dining room; drawing room; study; hall and downstairs loo. A mudroom for guns, dogs, muddy boots, and so forth, would be necessary as well, with a direct entrance from the outside. What would be nice? A kitchen large enough to have a good-size eating area with a fireplace. A large dining room with an equally huge table for when the family was here in mass. We could be as many as 30 on festive occasions, so we needed a large drawing room with plenty of room for everyone and a piano. And so I went about it, counting the windows that would be replaced and marking out where each room would be. The kitchen needed to be far away from the hall but close to the dining room, with a separate door to the outside for deliveries. Consequently, the kitchen and mudroom went on the courtyard side. The study and the downstairs loo were off the entrance, and the drawing room led into the dining room, with the kitchen across the corridor. It all linked up. Bob's your uncle! The staircase was the most difficult problem to solve. I had decided that in the mezzanine I would make small, pretty rooms for children and guests, but it needed to be connected to the rest of the house, and therefore return to the staircase in the hall. We finally did this by making an open corridor with a wrought-iron banister suspended across the hall and supported by two columns.

There was another major problem: four steel girders were necessary to hold up the new construction. They soared upwards from the foundations to the roof and, although they would be hidden on the second floor, they could not be in the drawing room. It was these that gave me my dimensions. I made them the focal point of the room by turning them into pillars and building around them. The double doors leading in and out of the drawing room were positioned between them. Again everything fell into place quite naturally. All building nowadays must be constructed according to seismic regulations. Here it was even more complicated because we were knitting the old with the new.

The second floor, or the top floor, was the bedroom domain. We have five children plus ourselves, so we needed six bedrooms. They were all keen to have a bedroom of their own. By now they were adults and earning a living, except for Olly and Vicky; it seemed logical. Looking towards the future, they would hopefully marry and need king-size beds. Do nothing by halves. I believe in the old motto, '*Chi piu spende, meno spende.*'[1] Beds are vitally important, as is sleep itself. A good bed will last forever, save medical bills by protecting the back and encourage natural, healthy sleep. We are all tall, big people and the correct mattress is essential. Michael, my brother, once mentioned when staying with me, that he thought his mattress 'was synonymous to cement'. 'One man's meat is another man's poison,' or let's say back. If you need a big bed, get the best and most

---

1. The more you spend, the less you spend.

compatible with the size of the room and the size of the sheets that can be bought commercially.

The kitchen was far below so we needed a small kitchenette for breakfast, flower vases, trays, the necessities for cleaning, and bathrooms. I put in a lift that went directly from the kitchen to the laundry room downstairs, connecting again. I didn't want to waste light so I constructed a central hallway from which all the rooms led off. Each bedroom had a dressing room and a bathroom. The dressing-room area was always as you entered to give breathing space and privacy to the bedroom itself. The shape and the size of the rooms decided, it was up to the children to choose their own and how they would particularly like them decorated – within limits of course.

I have described the three main floors from the courtyard upwards. Now we had the floors below. Directly underneath was the play area, as I have mentioned before, with the gym leading off the swimming pool area. Directly across the corridor I made a billiard room with a full-sized table and American-style bar in wood with a brass footrest and stools. The bar itself was an interesting find, it was originally a tax collector's desk. Very fitting for its future use! It is a cosy room with a fire and low lights. Next to this was a bathroom made to look like a library with books painted on the walls. The linen room was in this corridor too, which was an exact copy of Giovanni's above, and at the end by the stairs was Salvatore's cellar, dramatically featuring a wrought-iron gate. Directly around the corner is the staff apartment with its own entrance.

Down one flight of steps again there is another glass and wrought-iron door leading onto the swimming pool terrace and beside this, a kitchen with direct access to the dining area. Down again and we find ourselves in a garage opening onto the Borro Road and the cellar. That was it, not complicated, in fact it flowed and made sense.

The actual building and restoration of the villa took another two years, but this was my 'baby' and I had no difficulty in getting up in the dark, early hours of the morning and driving in the cold down the *autostrada* to the Borro. Every day was exciting, watching my dreams and plans gradually come to life.

With the structure finished, it was time to think about the floors. The three lower floors were easy: terracotta; traditional; simple; and easy to keep clean. The bedroom floors were laid with walnut in decorative squares with a lacquered finish, meaning no polishing necessary, just a wipe over with a damp cloth. On the ground floor I used oak, the same as the doors, again in decorative squares with an antiqued finish. I found these in Naples. They actually looked old and needed to be waxed and polished. In the kitchen, the floor was laid with large wide planks. This left me with the hallway, and Giovanni's corridor leading off it. I wanted to use French limestone, but it wasn't typical of Tuscany. I thrashed around, looking everywhere for a substitute. One of the most well-known places to find marble is at Massa Carrara, on the west coast above Forte dei Marmi. In desperation, I decided to go and investigate. I wasn't looking for marble, but there might have been another product, or a mixture of compressed marble dust that might have worked.

The family had had a house for many years right on the sea front at Forte dei Marmi. In the summer we would sail Ferruccio's dinghy and when looking back at the land, the great white scars of the quarries were very evident. As I drove down the *autostrada* those happy, sun-filled days came back to mind. How incredibly young we were. Where had all the years flown? The exit sign for Forte dei Marmi flashed up; on the spur of the moment I turned off and found myself back in the world of my youth. Very little had changed. It was winter and the beaches were empty. The shops, although mostly closed, seemed more prosperous and chic, but in essence the scene was the same. I imagined what it would look like in summer. The market in the main square, the pony rides, the famous 'Pietro' with his metal basket selling *schiacciata* on the beach. I parked on the sea road in front of the old house. It looked a little sad, shuttered and barred for the winter. There was the terrace leading into the *salotto*, where we would wait for lunch, famished from our morning on the beach. The whitewashed wall with the little gate was still there. Memories flowed over me. It was all so much the same, as if I had stepped into a time warp and gone back thirty years. I found myself smiling at the memory of one extraordinary incident that will always remain vividly in my mind. On that winter day, sitting in my car thirty years later, I was drawn back to that night as if it had happened only yesterday.

I was eighteen years old and it was a hot hot night in July. The pine trees around the back of the house were still, there wasn't a breath of wind as Ferruccio and I drove up to the house. It was nearly midnight and we had been out with American clients for supper. I wore a long white dress with thin diamante straps and high-heeled silver sandals. The dress was straight and moulded my figure. My skin was deeply tanned. As we approached the villa, shutters were flung open on the upper floor, and the head of Ferruccio's mother Wanda popped out. 'Ferruccio, Fulvia is not back, go and look for her and bring her straight home!'

It was Ferruccio's younger sister's birthday and as a treat she had been allowed to go, on her bicycle, to the famous

Capannina. The ambition of every young person in the area that summer was to go to the Capannina – a nightclub on the beach with a live band. It was the place to be seen. We turned the car around and started off again. When we arrived at the Capannina, Fulvia had already left. We turned around once again and started back along the sea road this time, keeping our eyes open for Fulvia. We turned onto a side road and there in the headlights was a penguin, a king penguin about 50 centimetres high. Ferruccio slowed the car but then made as if he was going to pass on.

'Stop, stop!' I cried, 'It's a penguin!'

'*Non, non, é una suora, non guardare.*'[1]

'You must, it will get killed in all this traffic!'

Reluctantly, Ferruccio stopped and I jumped out. I reached the penguin and tried to pick him up. He pecked me viciously on the hand and I smartly let go. The poor animal was making for the sea. There was, however, a large busy road with Saturday night traffic flying past between it and its goal. I followed the penguin's robust little figure with its black back and puffed out white chest, Charlie Chaplin-like webbed feet and tiny rubber black wings, as he struggled along at a waddle, lifting his head to the scent of the sea. I followed, tight white dress, brown body, with a waddle too. My movement was limited by the dress and high heels. Incredibly, we traversed the Belisha crossing in unison, penguin in front and me right behind. What a sight! Cars screeched to a standstill, people opened their car doors and stood gaping. What an amazing vision. A girl and a penguin, both black and white, waddling across the road, in the middle of a hot Saturday night by the sea in Italy. I imagine a few people's initial reaction was, 'I didn't realize I'd drunk so much.' As

1. No, no, it's a nun, don't look

the penguin reached the other side, I grabbed his rubbery wings from the back: this way he couldn't peck me.

'Darling, quick, open the car.'

'No way! You're not putting that bird in my car, put it in the boot.'

There was no alternative, he was heavy, so I did. Once back in the car, hand bleeding, Ferruccio asked me what I wanted to do with it.

'Take it to the *carabinieré*,' I replied. 'It must have escaped from somewhere.' We drove towards the main square, now deserted except for two unfortunate *carabinieré* on their motorbikes.

'Quick,' I said. 'Tell them we've got a penguin in the boot.'

'No way! You do it.'

So out I got and trotted around the car in my silver shoes and tight dress. 'Good evening, officer. I have a penguin in the boot I would like to hand over as lost property. We found him in the road.' No reply, just a steady stare. Then one of them sighed deeply and asked me if I knew what time it was. I said I imagined it must be nearing one o'clock.

'That's right Signorina, and it's time you went to bed.'

'Yes,' I said, 'I would like to go to bed but I can't leave the penguin in the boot.' It took some time to make them take me seriously, but eventually curiosity prevailed and one of the *carabinieré* got nicely pecked. We took the penguin to the *caserma*[1]. They could hardly take him on their motorbikes. Now that would have been a sight to see!

In the local newspaper the next day, there was an article describing the incident.

1. barracks

'Two young people find a penguin belonging to Agnelli.'

The Agnelli family did have a house two roads further down, but I never had the opportunity to find out if it was true, and how a penguin happened to be there.

I started the car and drove on to Massa Carrara, passing the *capannina* on the way. It was still there, still the same. It was a fruitless journey however, I didn't find what I was looking for, but it had been good to see Forte dei Marmi again.

I had decided to use the *pietra serena* for the door surrounds and the pillars in the hall, so this had to be brought through to create continuity. I finally decided to use untreated *travertino*, a risk, as it's delicate and marks easily, but there didn't seem to be any alternative. Large squares of *travertino* were patterned with small squares of *pietra serena*. Giovanni's corridor was in terracotta being a working area, with smaller squares of *pietra serena* continuing through.

I had imagined the stairs forming a romantic curve sweeping down into the hall. I could see my daughters in their wedding gowns gliding down in a haze of veil and flowers. It didn't work, it wasn't right, in fact, it was all wrong. It was completely out of character and it had to come down.

Mr Pacini was horrified. 'You can't take it down now, Signora. It's finished, you will ruin everything.'

'I will ruin everything if I leave it up,' I argued. The whole staircase didn't need to come down, just the end, which we made straight and simple. I made a costly mistake, but I'm glad I set it right and didn't just leave it.

We made barrelled ceilings in most of the rooms, though

not the mezzanine. A new experience for me, an interesting technique that is anything but an exact science. The base of the ceiling is flat in the usual way. A hook is then anchored in the centre and from this, fine metal bars are extended to the wall. Now is the time you have to make a decision you will live with always, you can't change this like curtain material. Standing, getting a crick in your neck, sometimes mounting a ladder in the middle of the room turning and twisting to get the feel from close to. If a room is not an exact square or rectangle, it takes many trips up and down that ladder. Once you have decided the curve you want, the rest is simple – though the plasterers have difficulty getting the depth even all over. It is a difficult position to operate in, but with time and patience, it works and all the trouble will have been worthwhile.

Mouldings were the next thing on the agenda. I went with the *architetto* to a factory in *collé val d'elsa*, on the way to Siena. It was a real Aladdin's cave. Finding someone to do the job was going to be difficult. I spied a little man who obviously knew his way around and went over to him. His name was Carlo or 'Harlo' as the Florentines would say.

'No, no Signora, I'm booked up for months.'

'I quite understand that, but seeing that you are here now, could you give us the benefit of your advice? Could you help me choose what would be correct for the environment I'm working in, I have no idea where to begin?'

The *architetto* wandered off with an amused smile. Harlo and I became friends. He had great experience and had just finished one of the major hotels in Florence. Together we enthused over patterns, discussed the height of ceilings, how chair rails should be placed, and in the end he agreed to come on site with samples we had chosen to explain how the work should be done. Pride won out and in the end he did the job himself. We remained friends, and he would turn up at unexpected moments and give me good advice on many aspects of decoration.

The structure and the basics were now finished, so the decoration began. The actual painting itself was easy, it was roughly a creamy white throughout. There were, however, special effects I needed an expert for. The *architetto* found me a gem, Gabriella Giorgi from San Giovanni Val'darno, not far away. We started with the kitchen, which was a combination of Giovanni's old office and the room next door joined together with an arch. While cleaning the ceiling and removing old paint we found here and there the remains of an intricate pattern, probably done with a type of stencil when the house was originally built in 1840. Only patches remained, but enough for Gabby to make a tracing and, in time, restore the whole ceiling to its original glory. I found old school lamps in a shop in Wandsworth Bridge Road and the effect was fabulous. You might say wasted in a kitchen but, on the other hand, it is the most used room in the house. The colours were brilliant, predominantly red and petrel blue. I decorated the rest of the kitchen around these colours, with cushions, tableclothes, pans and china. A kilim rug on the floor was a gift from Jamie. With the fire lit it was so warm and cosy, we spent a major part of our time here.

The large barrelled ceiling in the bedroom hallway created a far greater problem. This area had very little light, so I was going to use a *trompe l'oeil* to create it. We designed a balustrade around the ceiling cornice, a copy of the one in the garden with the same roses, a drape hung down in the corner in an apricot stripe. Barden, Ferruccio's dog, poked his head through in one corner, and there were two magpies for luck. In the centre, on either side, we placed a stone wall with mottos inscribed on them. Ferruccio chose one.

'*Le temps fait justice et met toutes les choses en leur place.*' – Voltaire.

Mine on the other side was more simple and came from the heart.

'Be sincere to yourself.'

In the middle was sky in brilliant blue, as it often is at the Borro with scurrying clouds and a flock of swifts. Every spring the swifts come back. I feel so bad when I see them trying to get back into places they have used for nesting over the years, but are no longer open. In the main garage, across the courtyard, I always keep the doors open at this time of the year, so they can nest. The cars are always covered in droppings but it is a small price to pay.

Gabby introduced me to a young man called Paolo Flori, the best marblist I have ever come across. It is his specialty and his work is phenomenal. Unless you actually touch the surface it is difficult to believe it is not real and even then, you are left with a doubt. He did two major projects for me, the most important being the columns in the drawing-room. I had searched high and low for mantlepieces, and never found what I wanted. Then all of a sudden I found two right there in Florence. One for my bedroom in white French marble, a masterpiece of carved swirls and love birds, and another 18th-century *scagliola* in a burnt orange colour, with oak leaves and acorns carved around the face. It seemed to fit as the floors and doors are in oak. Paolo turned the columns into authentic *scarriola* in the same colour. The second project was Jamie's bathroom. His room was very masculine with a huge Tudor-type bed in oak, which I had made in England. The colour scheme was green and I wanted to bring it through into the bathroom. Paolo made the upper part of the walls in green marble. This is a treatment I would always recommend. Although expensive, it's never as costly as the real thing; and it's eternal, completely water repellent and gives a wonderful effect.

A completely different type of painting was done for me by Domenico Mileto, who is a copyist. In the dining room 'Harlo' had made five large frames in plaster along the walls. I wanted to fill these with paintings of birds, architecture, palm trees and fruit, using soft, warm colours following through from the drawing room. I sketched out vaguely on the wall the palm trees and the architectural ruins, leaving him to create the picture. I gave him a famous book called '*Audubon's Birds*' and left the rest to him. The paintings were magnificent, just what I had hoped for. From these and their wonderful soft colours, I decorated the rest of the room.

The actual furnishing of the villa took almost another two years. The curtains and upholstery are not a long process once you have made a decision. I have a *tappezziere*,[1] Mr. Ferrini, whom I have known since the Forte dei Marmi days so we understood each other implicitly. I used materials from many different companies, some so distinct and recognizable that they are like old friends to everyone! Years before I used to go to the *cascine*[2] for shooting lessons, and one Tuesday, on my way home, I discovered a big market along the riverbank. One of the main attractions was the Scardigli stall. Here they sold furnishing fabrics. Today, they have a flourishing business. I don't go to the market any

1. upholsterer
2. park

longer, but to Monte Lupo near Empoli. They have job lots of materials from all over the world, the price is right, and with patience you can discover the most amazing fabrics.

The drawing room carpet was huge, nine metres by ten, and had to be made to order. I went to The Rug Shop in London's Lots Road. I chose wools in a marmalade colour, dull aquamarine, salvia and saffron yellow – the colours of nature. The design is a type of Herez, and the rug was made in India. It took months, I was full of trepidation and wondered if, after all this time, it would be right. Thank God, it was perfect! It had been washed with bleach to make it look old and the colours subdued. The very first night it was laid, red wine was spilled on it. No problem, as long as it's dealt with straight away and in the proper manner. It was the first of many spills, animal and human. I suppose it adds character.

Finding furniture is exciting and fun but it can't be done methodically. I looked everywhere I went. The best venue of course, is auctions. I find auctions feverishly exciting. England is full of them. I would buy the *Antiques Bulletin* and peruse it, marking off the possibilities, then for a week or ten days it would be a marathon from Yorkshire to Brighton. My sister-in-law Chiara, Massimo Ferragamo's wife, is an avid auction fan. Living in New York, she has plenty of scope. When she comes home after an auction Massimo will ask, 'Did you win anything?' He is right, going to an auction and getting what you want, bidding against other people, at the right price, is just like winning a prize. She pointed out to me a bed in a Sotheby's catalogue, a four-poster Imperial American belonging to Ralph Lauren. I love four-posters, but all the old ones are too narrow for other than single use. This one was huge, 221 centimetres long by 200 centimetres wide. Off we went. The sales room was packed. I sat in a state of nervous excitement through various lots with Chiara beside bidding for her own pieces. Finally my lot came up, the bed. The bidding started slowly. I watched to see how it was going, who was interested. Chiara gave me tips on who the people were – most of the men standing at the back were dealers. It was one of these who bid against me. We went up and up. 'Oh dear, I so wanted that bed.' My only hope was that he would have to sell it on. I wanted it for our bedroom at the Borro. I got it in the end. I broke a golden rule, however, and went over the budget. Having dealt with all the bureaucracy involved, I went to a favourite place, Swifty's on Lexington Avenue, to have a celebratory drink and to calm my shattered nerves. I needed some Dutch courage too. I had to tell my husband I'd gone over the budget. I walked down Fifth Avenue to the office with a mixture of feelings.

Massimo was waiting for me with a big smile on his face. 'You will never believe this, Mandy, a man has just called, he was caught in a traffic jam and didn't make the auction, and is offering double what you paid for the bed.'

Ferruccio looked at me. 'Sell it, it's a gift from heaven, how often do you go to an auction and come out twenty thousand dollars richer.'

'No!' I replied, 'You don't understand, it's the bed I want, not the money.' I'll never make a good businesswoman!

I once met a man from Reggello, now he was a jolly good fellow, so the rhyme goes, but he wasn't the man I was looking for, but someone far more precious, a restorer, Gastone Tognaccini. No ordinary *restoratore*, he taught restoration of fine painting at Florence University. A tall man with an easy smile and warmth that is contagious. His family is close knit, working together in a small business restoring

148

antiques, every member doing their own part. The youngest member is a young man called Gianfranco, very like his father, tall with a mop of dark hair.

I called Gastone and asked him if he could come over. He and Gianfranco arrived in their van early one morning. We walked through into the *salotto* which looked huge and empty. We needed bookshelves in the spaces left either side of the double doors by the *scagliola* pillars. The area seemed even bigger than usual.

'What do you think?' I asked Gastone.

'We'll never find an antique to fit this, and even if we did, with a few alterations and adjustments, you could look for years, and it would be enormously expensive. I suggest you have it made.'

I asked him if he could do it.

'No,' he replied, 'I'm not a cabinetmaker, I'm a restorer.'

Gianfranco looked at his father. 'I would like to try it, Babbo.'

I was surprised and delighted. With the help of the *architetto*, I came up with a design. Gianfranco hired part of a warehouse in Reggello, and got down to work. I wanted it in oak, old, if possible, or well-seasoned.

Gianfranco's courage in taking on this big project, using all the experience and knowledge he had acquired over the years working with his father, paid off. The bookcase was a work of art, admired by everyone who saw it.

He then took on Ferruccio's study decorating the walls entirely with wooden panelling, making inserts for the windows, plus window seats, and finally the mantelpiece. This room, too, is much admired. I bought a cabinet in walnut at an auction at Christie's in the Brompton Road. It had been converted into a drinks cabinet and was in very poor condition, so I sent it straight on to Gianfranco for restoration. I hoped to use it to keep the television in, but it didn't fit.

'I can copy it exactly if I can find the same old walnut,' Gianfranco said – and he did, changing the dimensions just enough to enable us to hide the television. You could hardly tell the difference. In Florence we are fortunate to have many artisans who make antiques, handles and knobs, and, of course, can copy anything.

Gianfranco has continued making furniture, but his real love is restoring antiques, just like his father, whose passion is the restoration of fine art.

The villa was almost finished, but I didn't want to move in until everything was perfect. In September there was a revolt; all the children took their belongings and moved over. I held out for a few days and then moved over too. We were in our new home. The home I had waited for so long.

That year we actually had Christmas in the new house, all the family came, 36 of us. The babies and small children were in the kitchen with nannies and high chairs, the fire glowing in the hearth. We were 24, sitting around the table in the dining room, with crackers, paper hats, sausages and bacon rolls. The drawing room wasn't finished, the sofas were uncovered and there was no carpet, but there was the grand piano. I had noticed an advertisement in a magazine for authentic antique pianos, restored to perfection by David Winston, an American who lived in Kent. I travelled down one afternoon with Ferruccio, and we bought a piano that had been played by Chopin, a Pleyel. An old piano never has the perfect mechanism or sound of a modern one, but not being a musician, it didn't bother me. I just loved the old wood, the patina, and its presence. I wonder what George Solti would have thought?

Our room is next to Jamie's, and it's my favourite room in the house. Large but comfortable, I could almost live up there. It has three large windows and two small oval-shaped ones. Like an eyrie, I can see everything from this corner. The village, the bridge, and I can call to Marta sitting on the wall outside her shop. All the garden is at my feet, I can see and hear the fountain, I can read my motto on the sundial. I can see who is on the Caccia Terrace and if Salvatore is in his office. I can hear the children on the swimming-pool terrace and see them having breakfast on the upper terrace in the morning. I can see and hear everything going on in the courtyard, who is arriving and leaving. I love this room, it's like the centre of my universe.

The American Imperial bed with its smooth mahogany pillars is the focal point. We made the canopy in white with a dark red binding and a green and red check lining. In the front of the fireplace there are two armchairs and a footrest in the same check material. I 'won' one of these armchairs at Phillips' Auction House on the Bayswater Road for £125. I had the second one copied. I made a dado all around the room at ninety centimetres high and then papered the rest. The paper is by Scalamandre, an unusual Chinese *toile* with bigger figures, lions and tigers, monkeys, and chinamen with hats and baggy trousers. The colours are alive and multiple on a white background, raspberry red, yellow and green, with an occasional glimpse of blue. We made the curtains in the same material with red trimming down the sides. The pelmets were long with a complicated pattern of appliqué done in the same trimming. I put a mirror over the mantle-piece that had once been the centre of a moulding. I had a pretty desk which I bought in Fiesole, and used it as a dressing-table with a beautiful Chinese-looking silver mirror I found in the Kensington Antique fair. Two glass lamps from the antique market on 26th and Avenue of the Americas in New York were placed either side. There was a bookcase lined in pale yellow silk, which I found in Brussels and a wheel-back chair, found in a warehouse in the Casentino, covered in the same pale yellow silk. I could go on, but it would be boring. Everything had a memory and a story for me. In the winter, with the fire lit, I could curl up in a chair and read or watch TV. In the summer I opened all the windows. High up in my corner the cool breeze would move in currents through the room and I felt part of everything around me.

19. *The dining room*

20. *Giovanni's corridor*

21. *The billiard room before work began*

22. *The billiard room after restoration*

23. *Entrance hall and staircase*

24. *Entrance to dining room*

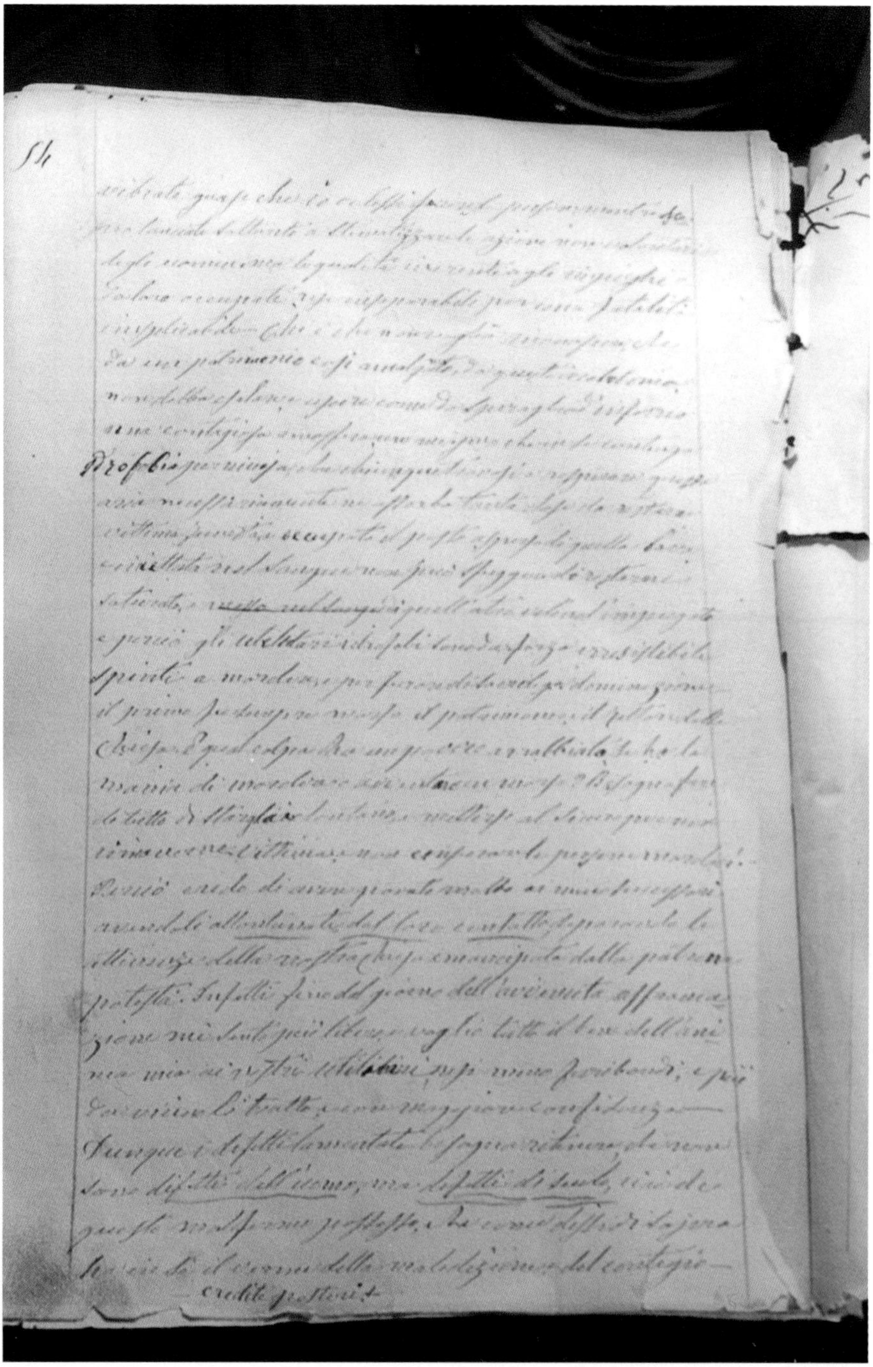

25. *Manuscript with the curse*

26. *Inside Borro church*

27. *The medieval festival — James (second from the left) and Salvatore (centre)*

28. *Poster of the festival*

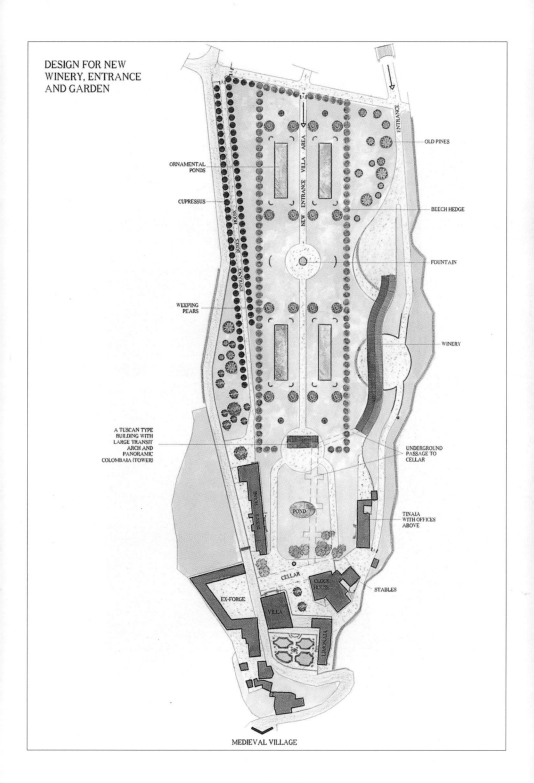

DESIGN FOR NEW
WINERY, ENTRANCE
AND GARDEN

OLD PINES

ORNAMENTAL
PONDS

CUPRESSUS

BEECH HEDGE

FOUNTAIN

WEEPING
PEARS

WINERY

A TUSCAN TYPE
BUILDING WITH
LARGE TRANSIT
ARCH AND
PANORAMIC
COLOMBAIA (TOWER)

UNDERGROUND
PASSAGE TO
CELLAR

TINAIA
WITH OFFICES
ABOVE

POND

CELLAR

EX-FORGE

VILLA

CLOCK
HOUSE

STABLES

MEDIEVAL VILLAGE

29. *The future plan*

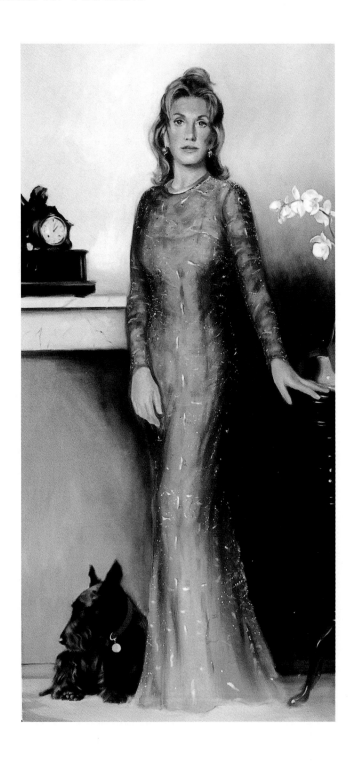

30. *Portrait of the author by Sophie Gilbert-Denham*

17 Ghosts and Spirits

'*Aiuto, Aiuto!*'[1] I could hear a muffled cry but I couldn't make out where it was coming from. Ghost stories were rife in the village, but I'd had no personal experience. I was on my own in the early evening of a winter's day. Leaving the warmth of the fire I went to investigate, walking into the dark hall. There it was again. '*Signora, Signora.*' A desperate cry followed by hollow knocking. Where was it coming from? I walked further into the hall, looking for the light switch, then stood still and listened. In the silence, suddenly, I heard it again, closer this time. '*Aiuto!*' I called out. 'Where are you?'

'*L'ascensore,*' (the lift), came the reply. Ah! No ghost, but Giuseppina Carruso stuck in the lift.

Giuseppina was responsible for the upkeep of the *agriturismo*, at that time, and as all the laundry was washed in the villa, had come to collect a change of sheets. Thank goodness I'd been there, it was late and there had been an unexpected guest. By sheer coincidence we had both been in the villa, when as a rule, we wouldn't have been. Giuseppina is a tough cookie and heaving a sigh of relief, we hugged each other and laughed. We had a sip of brandy in front of

1. help

153

the fire, to chase away any remaining demons, and Giuseppina departed with her pile of sheets.

A few evenings later I was describing Giuseppina's near escape from a night in the lift to Marta. 'This house is jinxed,' I joked. 'If it's not one thing, its another.'

She didn't laugh, instead she frowned. 'Of course it's jinxed, didn't you know?'

'I'm too prosaic for that type of thing,' I replied.

'This is a matter of facts,' answered Marta, and she told me the story.

There is a manuscript in the church archives here at the Borro, written by one of Don Pasquale's predecessors, Don Ferdinando Pieraccini. He lived in the 13th century, and at that time, the major part of the *poderi* around the Borro Estate belonged to the parish and the nuns at Montalcino, in other words, the church. The actual Borro villa and farm were then owned by the Medici-Tornaquinici.

The Tornaquinici insisted the church allow them to exercise their right of *padronato*, which allowed them to elect a parochial priest of their choosing. They chose their *cappellano di corte*, the court chaplain, Don Ciabatti, who was summarily sent to the Borro. A strange choice that then became clear. Through Don Ciabatti, the Tornaquinici bought the church lands at an *irrisorio*[1] price. Don Ferdinando Pieraccini was incensed and tried to retrieve the land, considering the whole deal a fraud. He was, however, unsuccessful.

I went to see Don Pasquale and obtained a copy of the manuscript. I quote Don Ferdinando's words:

1. paltry

Ghosts and Spirits

Questa malefermo possesso che no avra mai bene.
perche porta con se I segni della maladizione e del
contaggio.[1]

Vivia, my eldest daughter, in the first few months in the villa, said she had an uncomfortable feeling of another presence or spirit, and that her dog Bliza was edgy too. I never experienced this, and I think I can say the same for Bonnie; and yet it was in our room that an apparently unhappy incident happened, and a man fell to his death from the window.

There are many stories about Number 11 in the Borro, where Harvey Saks now lives. Which of course reminded me of Oscar Wilde's story, 'The Canterville Ghost.' Harvey has never had any problems, being an American, but a woman who lived there before declared that she would often wake up to find a woman standing by her bed, urging her to leave the house. Telephones have been heard to ring, lights seen to go on and off, windows found open. One, when there was no one in the house, and two, when there was no electricity. This was actually witnessed by a group of people having dinner in the restaurant, apart from other members of the village. Personally, I don't know what to make of it, as I have never had any first-hand experience.

Not long ago, I was reading '*Hannibal*' by Thomas Harris. I came to the part about Detective Pazzi, direct descendant of the old Florentine family, in the story of course, but the history is correct – it was an unfortunate family. Right here at Campo Gialli, just a small village now, only two kilometres from the Borro, there was in the 1300s a stronghold

1. This possession is damned and will never prosper because it carries with it a curse that is contagious.

155

of the Pazzi family, allies of the Borro and the Ghibellini. The castle was attacked by the Florentines in 1344. The victorious Florentines then hung 10 members of the Pazzi family at the gates of the castle. It seems that history was to repeat itself.

18 Il Borro a Casa, Weddings and Fairs

One of my favourite times is the end of the day, especially if you feel you've accomplished something. It's a good time to sit and think. I sat in my new drawing room, surrounded by its warm light and soft colours with the fire flickering, my hands around a hot mug of tea. Often Marta would join me and we would discuss the shop. What was selling well, and what wasn't. How we could improve the decoration. We sold so many objects it was almost like a bazaar: tablecloths, tea towels and laundry bags in a strong, coarse linen, printed with our own designs; pictures in rustic wooden frames, some pieces of furniture, ceramics, glassware, you name it, we had it. One of the bestsellers, however, were the silver and old linens I found at antique fairs on my travels. Wherever I was, in Portugal, America, France, or England, I'd search in nooks and crannies for interesting and unusual objects. We kept our prices low so as to be competitive.

When we first started the shop at the Borro we decided to make a line of our own produce; olive oil, vinegar and honey were the main items to begin with. Finding a logo was important. Rino, Elda's son, helped me with this. He was studying to be an architect, and eventually we came up with something simple and effective. An oval frame with a light sketching of the village in the middle and Il Borro written in bold letters on top. Fulvia, my sister-in-law, helped by having rolls of natural-coloured linen stamped with our logo. We would sit for hours with pinking shears, cutting it in to squares to place over the honey jars, tied with a coloured cord. The olive oil and vinegar were sold in the classic tall, squared bottles. Piled up on the shelves they looked very effective. We then expanded into jams and sauces, using Beppina's recipe. It all went so well we decided to open a shop in Florence, and I became the courier between the two, loading the car with merchandise in the evening and delivering it to the shop just before it closed at 7.30 p.m. I needed someone to run the shop in Florence, and my eldest daughter Vivia stepped in. The shop in Florence had to be more sophisticated than the one in the village. We sold Nina Campbell fabrics and, for a while, Blenheim carpets. Vivia started going to all the trade fairs and built up a large clientele. Our motto was 'value for money' and it worked.

The shop in Florence could not be run by one person, and so we employed Simonetta. The world is a small place: Simonetta was Angela's future mother-in-law. Tim and Angela had gone their separate ways, and now Angela was to marry Simonetta's son, Massimiliano Grecco. Of course, I was delighted, but it presented me with another problem I had been putting off for sometime, the Borro church. It definitely needed restoring and now the moment had arrived.

The roof was in fairly good condition; we didn't need to take down the wooden structure. The floor, however, I really didn't like. It had been laid with modern terracotta tiles. We decided to take it up. To our surprise, underneath there was another tiled floor, this time of compressed marble pieces. Under this we found the original, a beautiful old terracotta in a size no longer made today, but an ever bigger surprise was under this – two *sepulchre*; one still had an old rudimentary wooden coffin in it, fortunately empty. I wonder why! About a mile down the road from the Borro there is a brick factory. I had come across their work, which was still done in the *artigiano* way, at the Terranuova Fair. They agreed to remake the old tiles just as they had been at the end of the 16th century. We framed the *sepulchre* in *pietra serena* and heavy-duty glass, cleaned and lit them. Standing above in the central aisle you could look down into these ancient burial places. It was fascinating to feel the past coming back to life. The choir stalls at the back of the altar were remade in wood just as they must have been originally. The same with the confessional. I chose a dark red brocade curtain, to hide the priest, as a finishing touch. All the windows were mended or replaced. New pews were ordered and the walls replastered and painted. On either side there were two smaller altars, as you often find, and above each there was a stone frame, with nothing in it. I asked Don Pasquale what he thought.

'Two paintings,' he said, 'but of what?' The church is called San Biagio and he told me the story of the saint's life. How he had been a bishop and saved a child's life by taking a bone out of her throat, and of his terrible martyrdom by skinning alive. This sounded a bit gruesome, but we decided to copy two pictures showing these culminating moments in the saint's life. They are by no means masterpieces, but certainly add an interesting touch, and colour to the church. The last thing we did was renew the bell ropes. What fun it is to ring bells, but it's not easy. I can't imagine what the parishioners in San Giustino thought, when we tried them out. Bonnie and Briccola sat in the doorway and thought we were mad. The church was finished!

Being married at the Borro had always been popular, now it became a must. Don Pasquale was inundated with requests. Weddings mean receptions, which inevitably means eating and drinking. The restaurant was sitting waiting on the other side of the bridge at the bottom of the hill, so perfectly and conveniently located for just this purpose. When Marta and Gilberto gave up the restaurant it was difficult to replace them. Outsiders, meaning people from outside the Valdarno area, never made a success of it.

Il Cantuccio is San Giustino's pizzeria. The pizza is to die for, just the way I like it, thin dough with mountains of topping, crunchy and oozing with melted cheese. It was always crowded, especially at weekends. The two proprietors, Bruno and Giancarlo, are rather like Laurel and Hardy, one tall and thin, the other short and plump. They were ideal for the Borro restaurant. They had made such a success with Il Cantuccio, I was sure they could repeat this at the Borro. In the end, a compromise was reached. Bruno, small and plump, the *pizzaiolo*, would stay at the pizzeria and Giancarlo, tall and thin, would run the restaurant.

The restaurant itself was not well conceived. A pretty and unusual location, looking up at a medieval village, in the middle of beautiful countryside. It was the inside that was mismanaged, or, to be fair, was not ideal for a restaurant. It sat in the steep loop in the road below our garden wall, with a steep flight of steps running down the side. The back leaned into the hillside so the windows were mainly in the front looking towards the village. On the ground floor there was a large kitchen at the back, without natural light, the entrance from the veranda, a bar and a large stone fireplace. This left little room for tables. A steep flight of steps led up to the first floor. Here the windows had been enlarged into arches, which was out of character with the building, but

160

gave a lot of light and a great view. At night with the village subtly lit, it was magical. This dining area was quite large and at times it has been possible to sit up to 90 people. Behind this, off a small patio, a few steps led up to a good-sized terrace.

There was little I could do here without major alterations, which meant time. It wasn't that I didn't have ideas, they were just too big! As Ferruccio would say, 'Just an *auto-strada* here, and a flyover there'! So we did what we could with what we had. The terrace was relaid with stone slabs and a small, elevated area made into a special zone for a band. A flight of steps was made to connect this terrace with the veranda on the ground floor. About halfway down there is another small patio with a glass door leading from the main restaurant, where we planted roses, and rynchos-pernum, lemon trees and herbs in pots. It gave a feel of freshness and the herbs made all the difference to the cooking – clients could actually see them growing through the glass.

A marquee structure covers the terrace with a green and white striped awning in the summer, and Mr Fiacchini made us metal tables and chairs. On the walls around the terrace we planted *rynchospernum*, wisteria, and solanium with hydrangeas at their feet. In the middle around the base of an acer tree we had a border planted with acero, abelia and hebe.

On the inside we ordered tables and chairs to be made in wood. The tables were small and square, about one metre wide with a central leg. This enlarged the seating capacity and at the same time allowed for more intimate dining. For a large party, several tables could be placed together with no hindering legs which would make sitting uncomfortable. Marta made tablecloths in linen with our logo and a design of grapes printed in green. Simple white plates with our logo in green were also made to order. New light fixtures, combined with candles in silver holders with glass globes, gave a more romantic atmosphere.

Giancarlo devised an innovative menu with unusual dishes such as:

> Homemade Tagliolini with zucchini flowers and pine nuts
> Filetto of fine Beef slices finely with juniper berries and porcini mushrooms

But at the same time, typical Tuscan dishes were served also.

> Potato Gnocchi with Rucola Sauce
> Salmi of Capriolo
> Wild boar stew

The restaurant was, at last, ready for business. Business was good, very good. There were wedding receptions there every weekend from June through to October.

After about three years at the Borro, a group of people from the Terranuova Council suggested we have a band competition. 'What does a band competition consist of?' we asked. The Terranuova band was conducted by Orio Odori, who, apart from being a great conductor, was also a composer. He would compose an obligatory piece and the band or orchestra competing would choose a second one. The competition was advertised in the appropriate musical magazines and bulletins, after which a selection was made by a committee and the number of competitors reduced to eight. Bands were chosen from all over Italy, from Lombardia to Sicily. The organization was phenomenal: hotels, buses, and storage for instruments. The biggest question was where it could take place. The old forge yard was the only area big enough. The competition was fixed for March, which left me six months to restore it. Luciano Gori, assistant to the Mayor Carlo Pasquini, was doubtful. 'You'll never get it done in time.' I crossed my fingers and got down to work. The old forge yard had been used in recent years by a manufacturer of metal and aluminium frames, who had closed off the *loggia* with makeshift walls. It was a mess, and looked like a junkyard. Where to begin? With the obvious: clear it all out leaving just the basic structure, or what was left of it.

The roof was remade. By now we were experts, and the wonderful brick factory La Fornace di Baglioni down the road at the Laterina remade the bricks, as they had originally been, for the columns. So those that had been removed, or damaged, were restored or replaced. The floor was tiled with *klinka* and the courtyard itself covered in gravel. Lanterns were fixed on every other column and on those in between, hanging baskets in metal. The last thing we needed was coverage for the courtyard. The *architetto* designed a clever metal structure with Mr Fiacchini, the blacksmith. Each section was four metres by six metres and each one slotted into the next. We had an area of 400 square metres to cover. Being composed individually, we could use only what was necessary. Binding on the white plastic covering is a long boring job; when the whole area was covered, it could take as long as a day or two to put together.

We rebuilt the wall along the road, putting a wrought iron fence along the top, backed with cypress trees with long-flowering impatiens clustering around their trunks, happy in the shade on a hot summer day.

The job was finished just in time. There was space for 500 spectators with the bands under the *loggia*.

The day dawned beautifully, a real spring day, blue skies

and warm breezes. The baskets on the columns were filled with falling, variegated ivy with pink and white cyclamen in the centre. The vases on the Borro wall were filled to over-flowing with blue and white pansies. The irises under the robina trees made a carpet of blue, and the almond blossom in the valley was light pink snow drifting in the wind. The Borro was at her best and in a festive mood.

Each band gathered as their turn came, and there numbered between 35 and 50 instruments in the stable yard right in front of the horses' boxes. A last-minute practice and tune-up before going through the cellar and into the old forge yard. To begin with, the horses were nervous, whirling around in their boxes, their ears flat to their heads kicking out at the walls. As the day passed they calmed down and began to enjoy the commotion, especially the music.

The car park really came into its own: on this first occasion we had between 5000 and 6000 visitors. The cars lined the road as far as Campo Gialli.

The following May we had, by popular demand, our second edition of the band competition. This time Orio Odori conducted the two bands together, Terranuova and Loro Ciuffenna. He composed an obligatory piece called 'Amanda.' I was honoured, but, as I explained to the audience, it wasn't really an honour aimed at me as a person, but at the whole Borro. 'Amanda' means, literally translating from Latin, 'fit to be loved' and the composer, Orio, felt that it personified what he felt about the Borro. There was eventually a CD made to celebrate the occasion.

All the bands were very professional looking, in smart uniforms with distinctive badges, but I was completely unprepared for the music. It was truly beautiful. I sat entranced, and time flew by. We heard four bands in the morning. The Borro Ristorante catered for 1000 sittings for lunch that day, a record so far. Bruno and Giancarlo worked around the clock to make sure everything was perfect, and it was. In the afternoon another four bands played.

The judges had a very difficult decision indeed. Speeches were made, silver trophies awarded to winners and everyone was enthusiastic: 'We must make this a yearly event.'

The *loggia* courtyard opened up new possibilities for weddings. Giancarlo and Bruno now had space for more people sitting down. With help from Mr Matasoni, and Nila's genius with arranging flowers, candlelight and music, it was perfect.

Casa Detti is situated between the restaurant and the old forge yard, a difficult house to restore, basically because it was in a very ruined state, but also because, like the villa, it was built on a spur of land dropping steeply away to the Borro bridge below. The surrounding land was cracked and crumbling away, the earth itself friable and inclined to slide. We had faced the same problem with the Borro, and we solved this one the same way – armoured cement, camou-flaged with stones. It was a long job, but the only way to save the house and make it safe to live in. It was while working on this that I saw an arch, just a small half moon, in the remaining wall, on the more solid side near the road. Paccini was with me and I asked him to dig down to find out what was underneath. It was exciting. I waited with bated breath, the little digger worked away diligently, but progress was slow. It was not until the second day that we discovered a plaque with '1789' carved on it. Now I understood what it must be like to be an archaeologist, in a very minor way, of course. The excitement mounted as we continued to dig and a little cellar emerged, a gem in brick and stone with two arches leading into a little vaulted room behind. The floor was in stone with grooves for drainage. There was a circular millstone, to crush the grapes. It was a tiny cellar with all the necessities to make wine and store it. Whoever Mr Detti's predecessor was, he must have been a real connoisseur.

Having made the new retaining wall deeper and stronger, we recovered extra space for a larger terrace overlooking the Borro, with stairs connecting it to the garden below. Casa Detti, because of its position, had the same type of formation as the villa – three floors on the steep side facing the Borro and only two on the inner side. It is a pleasant house and we managed to close off a courtyard with a high wall, giving seclusion and privacy to the entrance, living room, and kitchen leading to it. The best part of this courtyard was an ancient fig tree we managed to save during the work, although it nestled right up to the side of the house. The big flat leaves gave shade and personality and a feeling of permanence that would have been lost without it. It was ideal for a family with small children. So we were especially pleased when it was rented to an Anglo-American family, with two small children and a West Highland terrier which, I might mention, became intimate with Bonnie! The father, James Suckling, was another author, a famous wine expert and writer for *Wine Spectator* and *Cigar Aficionado*.

There were many events held at the Borro, from doctors' conferences to fashion shoots in the villa and the garden. Many brides wanted to be photographed sitting by the fountain in the Italian garden. This became a sticky situation, the garden and the house were part of our private lives, and there had to be some limit – in the end we had to say no.

The biggest of all events, however, was the medieval fair. Around 13,000 people came over a period of one and a half days in the last weekend in August 1998. To be honest, I didn't enjoy this weekend. The crowds were suffocating, and the chaos continued until three in the morning with mead-drunk youths. The *architetto* constructed a tower in wood, which was painted and decorated with banners to look like the original entrance to the castle, with armed guards either side in medieval armour and chain mail with pointed metal helmets and nose plates. They must have been dying in the August heat. The whole Borro and restaurant was taken back to medieval times. There was no electric light: only torches or candles illuminated the alleys and *botteghe*[1], making the atmosphere suggestive and mysterious. Fires burned and wooden tables were laden with medieval fare, including the famous, or infamous, mead. There were fortunetellers, fire-eaters, and battles with troops in armour and heavy swords, dancing to chamber music, and games. We hired a company of well-known actors and artisans. They toured Italy doing these fairs and were, consequently, very professional. All the villagers, including children, and of course, Giancarlo, Bruno, and all the waiters from the restaurant, were congregated in the club above the shop, and kitted out in medieval garb. There was a lot of laughter and pointing of fingers, and, in fact, it was very amusing to see people you knew well transformed in hose and doublets, sausage-rimmed hats or veils with browbands. The best of all, though, were Salva and Jamie, forced under duress to don the medieval garb. Their strong, footballing legs were covered in woollen hose, and their outfits were completed with velvet pleated skirts and puffy sleeved jerkins, twinkle-toed shoes, and velvet padded hats – it was very difficult to keep a straight face. That Sunday they must have been photographed a thousand times. They gradually got into the part and became quite hilarious.

1. little shops

19 The Third Project

We have come to the third and last part of the project. The future plan for a 27-hole golf course, a golf club and hotel. We inherited this project from the Duke. It had been originally planned by the Studio Idea in Florence, complete with designs and maps. Now I started to weave my mind around it. The golf course part was not in my sphere of competence. I sat in on meetings with Ferruccio, Salvatore and Rino, Elda's son, who were working on it all together, principally, to understand the area involved and where strategically the hotel and club should be placed. This entire project depended on a tourist village, for a variety of reasons. A golf course is not, in any case until it becomes extremely well known and popular, a money-maker, in fact, just the opposite. The maintenance, if done properly, and an international championship course of 27 holes cannot be other, will cost in the region of £300,000 a hole, annually. A lot of money! Italy is not like America or England – golf is not, as yet, a very popular or a well-known sport. It is mostly tourists that play. Offering fully equipped apartments, with every necessity, that are pretty in a rural Tuscan setting, is more than important. It was the lifeblood of the whole plan. These were to be located a little out of San Giustino in the direction of Arezzo. The distance from us might have been quite substantial by road but as the crow flies, it was close to the villa on a spur of land just across the Valley of the Fairies. With prevailing winds, we would hear a lot of noise. With the planned fifty apartments, at full capacity, it meant 200 tourists. I was doubtful and worried, so when I was called to go and see Tito Barbini, the Assessore Regionale in Via Tournabuoni, the Florence headquarters of the region, with the architects and engineers from Idea, plus Elio Lazzarini and Salvatore, I was perplexed and nervous. We stood around together in the entrance talking in groups in low voices, no one was eager to sit down. There were strained smiles and not much conversation. This plan had been on the table for many years, and everyone had their own axe to grind.

We were ushered, en masse, into an adjoining room, where we waited again, tension building. The door opened and the Assessore Barbini came in. 'I only want *la Signora*, no technicians.' You can imagine how popular I was! I asked if Salvatore could accompany me and we went together into the office. Around a large table sat the Assessore, Dottore Sigone, Assessore of the province of Arezzo, and other important people involved. I knew most of them, but not well. I had met Tito Barbino at a conference we had given at the Borro on Il Recupero dei Centri Storici and just after that at a presentation of the Chimera d'Oro in Arezzo, which, being the symbol of Arezzo, was given to Ferruccio and I in recognition of our work at the Borro. It was a great honour. The ceremony was held in the evening in the San Francesco Square in front of the San Francesco church with the Piero della Francesca frescos; all the usual dignitaries of Arezzo were there. The Mayor and Valter Veltroni, Minister of Bene Culturale, now mayor of Rome.

Having introduced Salvatore, we sat down and Assessore

Barbini came straight to the point. 'I don't like the idea of all that cement.' He was talking about the tourist village.

'You are knocking down an open door, neither do I,' I said.

He drummed his fingers on the table in silence. 'Isn't there any old farmhouse or group of old buildings we could develop?' he demanded.

'Do you think I could have some coffee while I think?' I asked.

He smiled and we all had coffee while I put my brain in gear. It came to me, brain stimulated by the coffee – Monticello. This is a group of beautiful old buildings on the crest of a hill, with a vast view of all the Borro: the entrance to the villa; the airport; Alvaro's farm, where the riding school was; and Poggiano where the golf club was intended. A golfer would be in heaven, able to look down on a major part of the course. It was also divided by a road, that, by law, could be used by the public, so it was not particularly appropriate for a private house. This road led directly into San Giustino, coming out at the sports complex not 500 metres away, another enormous plus. It meant that we didn't take trade away from San Giustino but instead, augmented it considerably. Our tourists could actually walk into town, buy a newspaper and have coffee at Marisa's. If the complex was on the other site, it would have been too far. It really did seem a perfect location. Mr Barbini seemed pleased. 'Good, let's work on it.' In less than an hour I was back with the technicians, explaining the outcome of the meeting. It meant back to the drawing board for us all.

A few weeks later Salvatore came into my room carrying a sledgehammer, I sat up startled. 'What are you doing with that, darling?'

'It's what you are going to do with it, Mum, come with me.'

I hurriedly dressed and followed him, full of curiosity. Ferruccio had concluded a deal with the Duke to buy his house and his remaining land. The house, and the zoo with its lake, were all back in one property, unified and complete again. Salva wanted me to make the first dent in the wall.

'You made it, you take it down – it's only right Mummy.'

'I can't do that Salva, I won't be able to pick that thing up, let alone swing it.'

'Bend your knees, use your weight. Remember, you're a brown belt.' I was once a brown belt in Judo, many many years before, and I bent my knees and swung. I made the tiniest dent, and the vibration through my body nearly knocked me over. I tried again, and eventually made a pea-sized hole. Salva took over and did some real damage.

This new development meant we could start designing the new building for wine production. Ferruccio wanted it near the old cellar, so the wine, when ready to go in the *barrique*, did not have to travel. To begin with I had placed it at the far end of the zoo park, using the side entrance we had utilised on our first visit. I had no idea about wine production and had to find our how the mechanism worked.

The *architetto* drew up a large-scale design with all the surrounding area included: the villa, the Duke's house, the *tinaia* and entrances. We had our first meeting around the table in the new dining room. There was Stefano, now promoted to general manager, Salva, myself, Ferruccio, the *enologo*, Nicolo D'Afflitto and the *architetto*. The plan was spread out between us. The *architetto* did the honours and explained what we had in mind. The project was more his than mine. Ferruccio didn't like it. The new building was too far from the old cellar; it meant an enormously long tunnel to join the two. He had a point! We all looked at the map in front of us. There is a curve in the driveway near a side entrance by the little pink house. Here the verge of grass is much deeper. On the map it was clear. We could put the building there, it was considerably closer, on the other hand, we couldn't have the driveway trafficked by large lorries carrying wine, bottles, tractors, and so forth, but then this entrance led to the stable yard and the working area connected to the villa. What to do? I looked back at the map. The elegant part of the driveway with the symmetry of cypress trees and yew balls finished at the height of the zoo. What if I made a deviation, and cut across to the centre of the zoo park. From there I could make a new entrance in a direct line to the villa courtyard. Yes, it could work! I started to draw on the map. A long, straight entrance to the drive, broken in the middle by a rotunda and side paths, giving me four long narrow strips of land, two on either side of the drive. I drew rectangular ponds in each of these. At the end I placed a folly, not a useful building, something with an arch in the middle to give perspective. From this it would be possible to see the villa courtyard on one side, with the Italian garden below and the Borro village on the hill, and, on the other, the new Italian garden and entrance. It could work. We now had two entrances, one to the villa and the other to the working area.

20 The End of the Road

My seven years at the Borro were almost done. The year before, in June, we gave a big party for my mother and stepfather's 50th wedding anniversary. One hundred and thirty guests came from England. It was mad confusion the day before, 18 June – Mattesoni with his group of men going in and out of the house, the old forge yard decorated and draped with yellow silk, the San Giustino Band, La Tramontana and their pom-pom girls rehearsing a dance routine to Glenn Miller's 'Chattanooga Choo Choo'. Giancarlo organizing the kitchen and the table, candles and champagne and Massimiliano, the electrician, wiring up the lights. There were buses going to three different airports, and a fleet of taxis coming and going. The telephone rang incessantly.

My car was in continuous use, parked in the courtyard. By lunchtime we were all exhausted and for a short time there was a lull in the activity. The day was unusually hot and I was happy to escape to my cool room in the corner. Where was Bonnie? I opened the window and called for the umpteenth time. Nothing. The courtyard was empty, with just my car baking in the sun. Perhaps she has gone off to find her friends at Alvero's farm, the naughty girl. We had a rest and then the hive of activity buzzed relentlessly again. Around seven o'clock my brother Michael suggested we leave everything and go for a drink in the pub. Great idea! I went to fetch my bag collecting Christopher, my eldest brother, on the way. 'You coming with me? Let's go, we'll get there before the others.' I opened the car door and, there was Bonnie, her eyes looked at me, staring and glazed, her tongue hung out. 'Bonnie,' I whispered. 'Bonnie.' The branches of the trees swirled around me overhead. Screams echoed in my head. 'Bonnie ... Oh, Bonnie.'

Christopher's strong arms were around me lifting me up. 'Manda, don't.'

'Bonnie, I can't, I can't.'

They took me into the house and gave me brandy. I looked at my mother. Why, oh why didn't she bark?

I buried Bonnie next to the chapel and on her tombstone I wrote these words:

> Through bush of brow gleamed eyes of coal,
> With shining love from the depth of her soul,
> She crabbed and grimaced in a coy style,
> Unsheathing her teeth in a gummy smile.
> Patient she waited outside the bar,
> Always at my heel whether near or far,
> For better view on the armrest she'd sit,
> and only move when she saw fit.
> More loyal or trusting there never could be,
> That black bundle was part of me.
> Bonnie ... Oh, Bonnie, my very own,
> These few words are written in stone.

Bonnie left the Borro on the 18th of June. I left almost exactly one year later. But we'll be there in spirit always, both of us.

BEPPINA'S SPICY TOMATO SAUCE

1 pan about 22cm deep
1½ ounces of butter
1 medium red onion finely chopped
boiling water
1 wooden spoon
salt, one good pinch
3 cloves of garlic crushed
½ cup fresh parsley chopped
½ cup fresh oregano chopped
1 tablespoon olive oil
1 teaspoon sugar
1-litre tin of chopped or whole tomatoes
'Peperoncino' chilli freshly ground
½ cup basil chopped

Gently melt the butter in the bottom of the pan, heavy-bottomed pans are always best. Add the chopped onion and when it begins to absorb the butter, add a little boiling water and stir with a wooden spoon making a creamy mixture. Keep the fire low or you will burn the butter. Cook a few more minutes, the mixture must remain creamy not coloured; if it gets dry, add more boiling water. When the onion is cooked and soft add a good pinch of salt, along with the garlic, parsley and oregano. Stir well adding 1 tablespoon of olive oil and a teaspoon of sugar, and then pour on the tomatoes. Bring to the boil and let simmer for 20 minutes, the lid held open with the wooden spoon. Stir occasionally.

Just before the sauce is finished add the ground chilli, the amount depends on how hot you want it, and the basil. You must take the pan off the heat as soon as the chilli and basil are stirred in or the chilli will become bitter.

You can serve this sauce over any type of pasta or rice or use it over meatballs.

Source Index

International codes

Belgium 0032
England 0044
France 0033
Italy 0039
United States 001

The *Antiques Bulletin* – this contains details of every auction, market and fair worldwide
Tel 021 427 9440
    021 427 9333

Antique fairs, small objects in silver, prints, linens, and jewellery: London

Every Sunday in different hotels. My favourite is:
Park Lane Hotel
Piccadilly
London W1
Tel 020 7499 6321

Antique markets: England

Portobello Road and area
London SW11

Camden Market at Camden Lock
London N7

Antiques markets: Italy

Every first Sunday of the month
    Piazza Grande
    Arezzo

Every second Sunday of the month
    Centro Fiera Pistoia
    Via Sandro Pertini
    Pistoia, Florence

Every third Sunday of the month
    Fortezzo de Basso
    Firenze
    Or
    Piazza Centrale
    Lucca

Every fourth Sunday of the month
Piazza dei Ciompi
Firenze

Antique markets: New York

Every Saturday
    68th and York

Every Sunday
    77th and Columbus
    26th and Avenue of the Americas
    Broadways and Grand Street

Source Index

Antique markets: Paris

The magazine to buy is *Aladin*
For information see
www.pariscope.fr/cgi.o2/SalonHome

Marche Aux Puces de la Porte de
Vauves

Marche aux Puces de la Porte de
Montreuil

Les Puces de Saint Oven

Antique restoration and reproduction

Mrs Rosie Ford
Serendipity
The Tythings
Preston Court near Ledbury
Herefordshire
England
HR8 2LL
Tel 01531 660245

Gianfranco Tognaccini
217 Via Alighieri Dante
Regello
Firenze 50066
Italy
Tel 055 869083
Cell 328 375 8196

Antiques Shops Brussels

Galeries de Minimes
23 Rue des Minimes
1000 Bruxelles
Belgium
Tel 02 511 28 25
Fax 02 511 2825

La Crocade du Sablon
25 Rue des Minimes
1000 Bruxelles
Belgium
Tel 02 511 7993

Village des Antiquaries
22 Rue de Bodenbroek
1000 Bruxelles
Belgium
Tel 02 511 22 42

Antiques shops: Florence

Via Maggio and Via dei Fossi are
almost exclusively dedicated to
antiques of top quality

Il Cortile Fossombroni (this is more
varied and less expensive)
7R Via dei Rossi
Firenze 50123
Italy
Tel 055 287683
Fax 055 287683

Antique shops: New York

Hooksick Antiques Center
New York Route 7
Troy Bennington Rd
Hooksick
New York, NY 12089
Tel 518 686 4700

Antique shops: United Kingdom

The Furniture Caves
533 Kings Rd
London
SW10 L2Z
First Floor
Tel 020 7352 2046

14 shops in one building, including:
  Phoenix Trading Co.
  Tel 020 7351 6543

June Metcalf
Tel 020 7351 0400

Jean Brown Antiques Ltd.
Tel 020 7352 1517

The Anthony Redmile Collection
Tel 020 7351 3813
Fax 020 7352 8131

The Old Cinema Antiques
160 Chiswick High Rd
London W4 1PR
Tel 020 8995 4166
Fax 020 8995 4167

157 Tower Bridge Rd
London SE1 3LW
Tel 020 7407 5371
Fax 020 7403 0359

Lassco Architectural Antique Salvage
St Michael's Church
Mark St
London EC2A 4ER
Tel 020 7739 0448
Fax 020 7749 9941

Architects

Studio Architetto Ello Lazzarini
11 Via Rossini
Gioacchino Giustino Valda
Arezzo 52024
Italy
Tel 055 977874
Fax 055 977874
e-mail eljolazzarino@leonardogroup.it
website www.leonardogroup.it

Auction houses: England

Bonhams Auctioneers
Montpelier St
London SW7 1HH
Tel 020 7393 3900

65/69 Lots Rd
London SW10 0RN
Tel 020 7393 3900

Philips Auctioneers
101 New Bond St

London W1S 1SR
Tel 020 7629 6602

10 Salem Rd
London W2 4DL
Tel 020 7313 2700

Sotheby's Auctioneers
34 New Bond St
London W1A 2AA
Tel 020 7293 5000

Christie's Auctioneers
8 King St
London SW14 6QT
Tel 020 7839 9060

85 Old Brompton Rd
London SW7 3LD
Tel 020 7581 7611

Tennants
The Auction Centre
Lyburn
North Yorkshire DL8 58G
Tel 01969 623 780
Fax 01969 624 281
e-mail enquiry@tenants-ltd.co.uk
www.tenants.co.uk

Auction houses: New York

Phillips Auctioneers
406 East 79th St
New York, NY 10021
Tel 212 570 4830

Christie's
20 Rockefeller Plaza
New York, NY 10020
Tel 212 636 2000

Sotheby's
1334 York Avenue
New York, NY 10021
Tel 212 606 7000

Source Index

William Doyle Gallery
175 East 87th St
New York, NY 10028
Tel 212 427 2730

Tag Sale
University Place
Between 13th and 12th St Eastside
New York

Awnings

Alvaro Glovannetti
13 Via Rocca Tedolda
Firenze 50136
Italy
Tel 055 6503923
Fax 055 6505512

Bathrooms, tiles, taps etc.

Sivico Firenze srl
29F-31A Via Maragliano
Firenze 50144
Italy
Tel 055 36 051
Fax 055 363 146
e-mail mc8248@mclink.it

Capaccioni
19 Via Filippo Turati
Loro Ciuffenna
Arezzo 52024
Italy
Tel 055 917 2007

Ricardo Barthel
234R Via de'Serragli
Firenze 50124
Italy
Tel 055 228 0721
Fax 055 222 286

C.P. Hart
Newnham Terrace
Hercules Rd

London SE1 7DR
England
Tel 020 7902 1000
Fax 020 7902 1001

Beds

And So to Bed
638/640 Kings Rd
London SW6 2DU
England
Tel 020 77731 3593
www.andsotobed.co.uk

Simon Horn
117-121 Wandsworth Bridge Rd
London SW6 2TP
England
Tel 020 7731 1279
Fax 020 7736 3522

Blacksmiths

Fiacchini Angiolino snc
5 Via Silvio Pellico
Loro Ciuffenna
Arezzo 52024
Italy
Tel 055 977571

Bonarini
Frazione Vitereta
Laterina
Arezzo 52020
Italy
Tel 0575 89006

Bricks made to measure

Bagloni srl
37 Via Valdascione
Laterina
Arezzo 52020
Italy
Tel 0575 89009
Fax 0575 894609

Source Index

Carpets

The Rug Company
124 Holland Park Ave
London W11 4VE
England
Tel 020 7299 5148
Fax 020 7792 3384
www.rugcompany.co.uk
e-mail info@rugcompany.co.uk

Blenheim Carpets
51 Beauchamp Place
London SW3
England
Tel 020 7225 3393
Fax 020 7225 0440

Tappeti Afshan srl
4/6 Via Guido Monaco
Arezzo 52100
Italy
Tel 0575 22227

Contractors

Edilizia Pacini srl
12 Via Mazzini
Terranuova Bracciolini
Arezzo 52028
Italy
Tel 055 973 8727

Doors and windows

Donatello Fabroni Effedi snc
Localita Botriolo
Castlefranco di Sopra
Arezzo 52020
Italy
Tel 055 9149149
Fax 055 9149149
e-mail effedi@val.it

Lassco Architectural Antique Salvage
St Michael's Church

Mark St
London EC2A 4ER
England
Tel 020 77390448
Fax 020 7749 9941

Electrician

Technoluca
21 Via XI Febbraio
San Giovanni Valdamo
Arezzo 52027
Italy
Tel 33 88388579
Fax 33 88388573

Fabrics outlet – inexpensive

Scardigli & Ghini
133/137 Via Sottopoggio
Localita Villanova
Empoli, Firenze 50053
Italy
Tel 0571 993330
Fax 0571 993330

Beckenstein Fabric and Interiors
4 West 20th St
New York, NY 10011
USA
Tel 212 366-5142
    212 475-4887

Silk Surplus New York
1127 2nd Avenue
New York, NY 10022
USA
Tel 212 753-6511

Frames

Alpi
40R Via Toscanella
Firenze 50125
Italy
Tel 055 282920

Source Index

Furniture built in or made to measure

Donatello Fabroni Effedi snc
Localita Botriolo
Castlefranco di Sopra
Arezzo 52020
Italy
Tel 055 9149149
Fax 055 9149149
e-mail effedi@val.it

Serafini
S.D. Mobili Di Serafini Enrico & Co.
  snc
266 Via Sette Ponti
Quarata
Arezzo 52040
Italy
Tel 0575 364202
Fax 0575 364706

C.S. Falegnameria di Vivarelli
Graziano
150/152 Via Giusti Giuseppe
Calenzano
Firenze 50014
Italy
Tel 055 8878950
Fax 055 8878950

Sophisto Cat-Pine Furniture
188-192 Wandsworth Bridge Rd
London SW6 2VF
England
Tel 020 7731 2221
Fax 020 7731 0802

Yeoward
The Old Imperial Laundry
71 Warriner Gardens
London SW11 4XW
England
Tel 020 7498 4811
Fax 020 7498 9611
e-mail wy@yeowardsouth.com

Garden Furniture & Architectural Works and Fireplaces

2nd Avenue between 70th and 60th St
New York, NY
USA
Tel 212 941 4800

King's Antiques Corps
47 East 11th St
New York, NY
USA
Tel 212 674 2620
   212 253 6000

Lassco Architectural Antique Salvage
St Michael's Church
Mark St
London EC2A 4ER
England
Tel 020 7739 0448
Fax 020 7749 9941

Floors in wood, tiles, terracotta

Sivico Firenze srl
29F-31A Via Maragliano
Firenze 50144
Italy
Tel 055 36 051
Fax 055 363 146
e-mail mc8248@mclink.it

Capaccionli
19 Viale Filippo Turati
Loro Ciuffenna
Arezzo 52024
Italy
Tel 055 917 2007

Floor treatment, staining, polishing and cleaning

Girolami
24 Viale Giotto
S. Giovanni Valdarno

Source Index

Arezzo 52027
Italy
Tel 055 940107

Garden

Paolo Matasoni
94 Via Vespucci
Montevarchi
Arezzo 52025
Italy
Tel 055 982260

Garden furniture and ornaments

Garden Ornaments Stone srl
82 Via Cordellina
Sovizzo 36077
Italy
Tel 0444 370111
Fax 0444 370310

Lassco Architectural Antique Salvage
St Michael's Church
Mark St
London EC2A 4ER
England
Tel 020 77390448
Fax 020 77499941

Unopiu Europa spa
69B Via Fratelli Cervi
Capalle-Campi Bisenzio
Firenze 50013
Italy
Tel 055 89 85 935
Fax 055 89 85 935

Emporio S. Firenze
Ciani
9.14 Piazza S. Firenze
Firenze 50122
Italy
Tel 055 213235-210079
Fax 055 642826

Fiacchini Angiolini snc
5 Via Silvio Pellico
Loro Ciuffenna
Arezzo 52020
Italy
Tel 055 977571

E.M.U. Garden Furniture
97 Viale 20 Settembre
Sesto Florentino
Firenze 50019
Italy
Tel 055 44 33 03
Fax 055 44 55 18

Glass, decorative, housewares

Locchi
10 Via Burchiello
Firenze 50124
Italy
Tel 055 2298371
Fax 055 229 418

Handles of all types, key holes, etc.

Ferramenta Florentina
71a Via Del Cantone
Sesto Florentino
Firenze 50019
Italy
Tel 055 316954

Fratelli Bartollini snc
16 Vicchio, Via Macelli
Firenze 50039
Italy
Tel 055 84 4362

Rafanelli
7R Via del Sole
Firenze 50123
Italy
Tel 055 283 518

Giusti & Bandinelli
55R Via Palazzuolo
Firenze 50123
Italy
Tel 055 217878
Fax 055 217878

Interior decoration

Cullman & Kravis Inc.
Suite 206
790 Madison Ave
New York, NY 10021
USA
Tel 212 249 3874
Fax 212 249 3881

Imogen Taylor, The Interior Design
Studio
85 West Bourne St
London SW1 8HF
England
Tel 020 7823 4101

Colin Orchard Consultants
336 Kings Rd
London SW3 5OR
England
Tel 020 7352 2116
Fax 020 7351 9469

Nina Campbell
9 Walton St
London SW3 2ID
England
Tel 020 4225 1011
Fax 020 7225 0644

Kitchens

Ricardo Barthel
234R Via Serragli
Firenze 50124
Italy
Tel 055 228 0721
Fax 055 228 0721

C.S. Falegnameria di Vivarelli
Graziano
150/152 Via G. Giusti
Calenzano
Firenze 50014
Italy
Tel 055 8878950
Fax 055 8878950

Serafini
S.D Mobili Di Serafini Enrico & Co.
snc
266 Via Setteponti
Arezzo 52040
Italy
Tel 0575 364202
Fax 0575 364706

Donatello Fabroni Effedi snc
Castlefranco di Sopra localita Botriolo
Arezzo 52020
Italy
Tel 055 9149149
Fax 055 9149149
e-mail effedi@val.it

Lighting

The Anthony Redmile Collection
533 Kings Rd
Chelsea, London SW10 0T2
England
Tel 020 7351 3813
Fax 020 7352 8131

Soprasotto Lampshades
15 Via Buonarroti Michelangiolo
Firenze 50122
Italy
Tel 055 2469 083
Fax 055 2260 976

Vaughan Ltd
Chelsea Harbour Design Centre

London SW10 0XE
England
Tel 020 77349 4600
Fax 020 77239 46156
e-mail vaughanlighting.co.uk

Finch & Fryer Lighting
88 Wandsworth Bridge Rd
London SW6 2TF
England
Tel 020 7731 8888

Fergus Cochrane Leigh Warren
570 Kings Rd
London SW6 2D4
England
Tel 020 7736 9166
Fax 020 7297 2508

Mariotti S.A.S. Lampadari Artistici
9 Via S. Spirito
Firenze 50100
Italy
Tel 055 283300
Fax 055 977864

Charles Edwards (Antiques) Ltd
582 Kings Rd
London SW6 2D4
England
Tel 020 7736 8490
Fax 020 7351 5436

Emporio S. Firenze
Ciani
9.14 Piazza S. Firenze
Firenze 50122
Italy
Tel 055 213235-210079
Fax 055 642826

Oriental Lamp Shade Co.
816 Lexington Ave
New York, NY 10021

USA
Tel 212 832 8190

223 West 79th St
New York, NY 10024
USA
Tel 212 873 0812

John Rosselli Ltd
255 East 72nd St
New York, NY 10021
USA
Tel 212 737 2252
Fax 212 737 8819

Cecchi Mario Lighting
2 Via S. Elisabetta
Firenze 50122
Italy
Tel 055 294520

Tindle
168 Wandsworth Bridge Rd
Fulham
London SW6 2VQ
England
Tel 020 7384 1485
Fax 020 7736 5630

Wonderful Lamps – Besselink & Jones
99 Walton St
London SW3 2HH
England
Tel 020 584 0343
Fax 020 7584 0284

Mantlepiece

Galleria Ugo Camiciotti
9R Via S. Spirito
Firenze 50125
Italy
Tel 055 294837
Fax 055 2398072
e-mail pgrcam@tin.it

Source Index

Mouldings

Jago Rovai
Colle di Val'd'elsa
Siena 53034
Italy
Tel 0577 920441

Old Masters

Baumkotter Gallery
63A Kensington Church St
London W8 4BA
England
Tel 020 7937 5171
Fax 020 7938 2312

Painting specialists

Paolo Flori Stucco and False Marble
13 Via Antonio Vivaldi
Calenzano
Firenze 50041
Italy
Tel 335 825 8850
Fax 055 8827617

Giancarlo Tinti
22 Via Roberto Rossellini
San Giovanni Valdamo
Arezzo 52027
Italy
Tel 348 604603

Gabriela Giorgi trompe l'oiel
3 Via P. Arentino
Figline Valdamo
Firenze 50063
Italy
Tel 335 663 6726
Fax 055 9155 450
e-mail giorgi@firenze.net

L'arcimboldo
Studio d'arte di Domenico Mileto
18 Via Del Crocino

Loc Poggio alla Croce
Greve in Chianti
Firenze 50020
Italy
Tel 055 8337925
Fax 055 8337925
Cell 335 5424336
e-mail info@studioarcimboldo.com

Plumber

Silvano & Mauro Falsetti
Effe Implanti snc
85 Via della Chimera
Arezzo 52100
Italy
Tel 0575 302104

Piano

David Winston
England
Tel 01580 291 393
Tel 01580 241 872

Plaster

Giovanni Caruso
46 Via Frazione di Campogialli
Terranuova Bracciolini
Arezzo 52020
Italy
Tel 055 977910
Cell 348 2490661

Pictures and prints

Ramsay Prints
The Old Imperial Laundry
71 Warriner Gardens
London SW11 4XW
England
Tel 020 7720 2096
Fax 020 7622 4550

Source Index

Nencioni Wanda, Prints and Frames
25R 34R 36R Via Codnotta
Firenze 50122
Italy
Tel 055 215 345
Fax 055 281 202

Photographer

Foto Studio la Galleria di Sergio
  Piccioll
2331 Via Lungamo
Terranuova Bracciolini
Arezzo
Italy
Tel 055 9737412

Roses

Rose Barni
5 Via del Casello
Pistoia 51100
Italy
Tel 0573 380 464
Fax 0573 382 072
e-mail info@rosebarni.it
www.rosebarni.il

Silver

The London Silver Vaults Ltd
Chancery House
Chancery Lane
London WC2A 1QS
England
Tel 020 7242 3844

Paglial Silver Antiques and Repair
41R Borgo San Jacobo
Firenze 50125
Italy
Tel 055 282 840

Stone and marble

Dell Eugenio Roberto snc
69 Strada Statale no. 22
San Giovanni Valdarno

Arezzo 52027
Italy
Tel 055 9123095
Fax 055 944271

Terracotta garden ornaments and pots

F.III Centi snc
49 Via Concini
Terranuova Bracciolini
Arezzo 52028
Italy
Tel 055 9199835

Trimmings

Valmar
53R Via Porta Rossa
Firenze 50100
Italy
Tel 055 284 493

Wendy Cushing Trimmings Ltd
116 Middleton Rd
Dalston
London E8 4LP
England
Tel 020 7249 9709
Fax 0207 241 3441

Upholstery

Fui Ferrini snc di Lucchi Iandrea & Co.
15R Via Sacchetti
Firenze 50133
Italy
Tel 055 583627
Fax 055 583627

Wood, carving and decorative

Castorina
1315R Via S. Spirito
Firenze 50125
Italy
Tel 055 21 28 85
Fax 055 26 50 504

Index

189

Index

Index

Index

Index